# Praise for *Motherland*

'*Motherland* had me feeling angry, then sobbing, then laughing, then cheering and finally left me so inspired. These true stories, captured so beautifully by Stephanie Trethewey, reveal the guts, grit and courage of rural women while celebrating the power of the human spirit when adversity arrives. A must-read for all women.' **Maggie Dent, bestselling author of *Girlhood* and *From Boys to Men***

'I absolutely loved this book. I laughed, I cried and, thanks to Steph's talented storytelling, I feel bonded to the women of the land she has highlighted so honestly.' **Giaan Rooney, Olympic swimmer, television presenter and farmer**

'Stephanie Trethewey's debut book, *Motherland*, offers us a very rare and personal insight into the brave and unique lives of Australian rural women—what a privilege.' **Bridie Carter, actor**

'*Motherland* is a love letter to rural Australia. It's raw and real. What you read here is life in rural Australia and I'm so glad there these stories are out there.' **Fleur McDonald, bestselling Australian author, Voice of the Outback**

'What started as a way to connect lonely mums across the land has evolved into a touchstone of inspiration, friendship and camaraderie with a whirlwind of emotions thrown in.' **Catriona Rowntree, *Getaway* presenter**

**Stephanie Trethewey** is an accomplished broadcast journalist who spent more than seven years as a TV reporter and producer for some of the country's biggest news and current affairs programs.

Stephanie is the founder and CEO of Motherland, an organisation that's on a mission to eliminate the crippling isolation faced by many rural mums across Australia. Through the Motherland podcast, rural women share their extraordinary stories of motherhood on the land; over the past three years, Stephanie has interviewed more than 200 rural mums.

In 2022, Stephanie was named Australia's AgriFutures Rural Woman of the Year for her work improving postnatal support services for rural mums through Motherland Village, Australia's first personalised online rural mothers' group program.

Stephanie lives in Tasmania with her husband Sam and their two young children Elliot and Evie. Together, they run a regenerative food business, the Tasmanian Agricultural Company, from their family farm.

STEPHANIE TRETHEWEY

# MOTHER LAND

ALLEN&UNWIN
SYDNEY • MELBOURNE • AUCKLAND • LONDON

First published in 2023



Some names and identifying details have been changed to protect the privacy of individuals.

Allen & Unwin
Cammeraygal Country
83 Alexander Street
Crows Nest NSW 2065
Australia
Phone: (61 2) 8425 0100
Email: info@allenandunwin.com
Web: www.allenandunwin.com

*Allen & Unwin acknowledges the Traditional Owners of the Country on which we live and work. We pay our respects to all Aboriginal and Torres Strait Islander Elders, past and present.*

NATIONAL LIBRARY OF AUSTRALIA

A catalogue record for this book is available from the National Library of Australia

ISBN 978 1 76106 603 0

Map by Mika Tabata
Set in 12/20 pt Adobe Caslon Pro by Midland Typesetters, Australia
Printed and bound in Australia by the Opus Group

10 9 8 7 6 5 4 3 2 1

FSC www.fsc.org MIX Paper | Supporting responsible forestry FSC® C001695

The paper in this book is FSC® certified. FSC® promotes environmentally responsible, socially beneficial and economically viable management of the world's forests.

I would like to acknowledge the Australian Aboriginal and Torres Strait Islander people, the traditional custodians of the land we live on. I want to pay my respects to ancestors and Elders, past, present and emerging, and I especially want to acknowledge the Palawa people, who are the traditional owners of my incredible island home, Lutruwita. I recognise our First Nations peoples' continuing connection to land, waters and community. We have so much to learn from them as the world's oldest continuing culture.

*For the Motherland community.*

*And for the loves of my life, my darling Sam, Elliot & Evie.*

# Contents

# Motherland Mothers and Where They Live

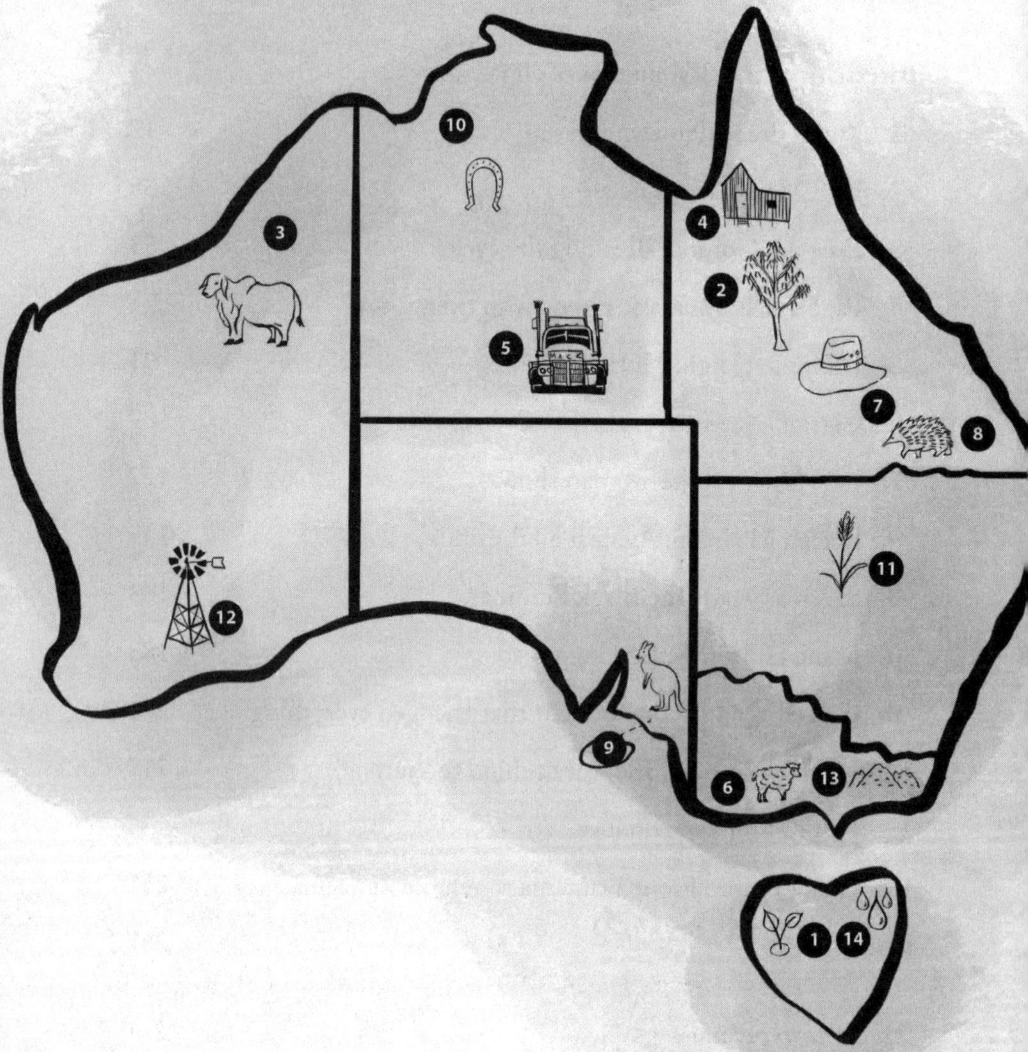

# MAP KEY

1
KAREN BROCK:
Meander Valley, TAS

2
JULIE McDONALD
Devoncourt Station, QLD

3
DARRYLIN GORDON
Kimberley, WA

4
PAT FENNELL
Mount Isa, QLD

5
DANYELLE HAIGH
Anmatjere, NT

6
CATRIONA ROWNTREE
South-west, VIC

7
JULIE MAYNE
Dulacca, QLD

8
KEELEN MAILMAN
Mount Tabor, QLD

9
SABRINA DAVIS
Kangaroo Island, SA

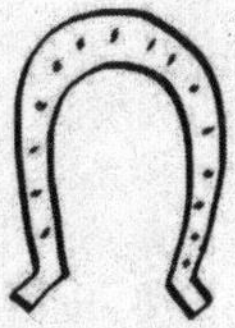
10
RAINE HOLCOMBE
Timber Creek, NT

11
GRACE BRENNAN
Warren, NSW

12
FLEUR McDONALD
Esperance, WA

13
LYN KELSON
Drummond, VIC

14
DIANA BUTLER
Launceston, TAS

# Introduction

# The mother of all journeys

The fact I've managed to write this book is nothing short of miraculous. While my journey through motherhood is the very reason it exists, ironically, being a mum is also what made this project near impossible. Turns out penning coherent sentences when you're exhausted from raising two small humans is no mean feat.

As I type this on my laptop in our living room, which overlooks the farm, my little girl Evie is lying on the floor gazing contentedly up at me and my son Elliot is standing at the window and literally, and very enthusiastically, counting cows aloud. My environment and my new home still feel surreal at times and to say my life has taken an unexpected twist in recent years would be an understatement.

I've gone from being a national TV reporter who chased criminals through the streets of Melbourne to mustering cattle and raising two kids in country Tasmania. The change from TV journalist to rural mum might sound charming, but my transition to life on the land has at times nearly broken me. However, at its core, this new reality has ignited an unexpected fire in my belly and an unwavering desire to tell the incredible tales of rural mothers across the country.

> The change from TV journalist to rural mum might sound charming, but my transition to life on the land has at times nearly broken me.

A born-and-bred Sydney girl with a thirst for the bright lights of the city and the adrenaline rush of a newsroom, I never gave a second thought to life in rural Australia or to the women in it; I was too busy cursing traffic. My world revolved around stakeouts, script deadlines and the stress of live TV. Climbing the ladder and doing whatever it took for my reporting career to flourish was my life's sole purpose. That is, until I fell in love with a very handsome farmer.

It was 2013, and at the time I was based in Rockhampton managing Channel Seven's Central Queensland newsrooms as reporter and producer. Sourcing the news each day for the 6 pm evening bulletin was my responsibility and Rocky could get a little sleepy from time to time. One muggy December morning, I still vividly recall literally sweating as I scrambled to find another story to fill the bulletin; I was in the middle of a story drought—every journalist's worst nightmare. I'd read the newspapers, phoned my police contacts, contacted council and sifted through my little black book. Nothing. There'd been no car accidents, no serious crimes committed, no politicians in town and no significant announcements. Rockhampton was dead, but, as it turns out, love wasn't.

As a last resort and desperate for a story, I dragged my cameraman along to a local agriculture event being held in town. The guest speaker was a young farmer from Tasmania named Sam Trethewey and not only did I manage to squeeze a decent story out of my interview with him, I also nabbed myself a boyfriend in the process. This chance meeting with my future husband set my soul (and my ovaries) on fire and kicked into motion a chain of events that would change the course of my life forever. Little did I know that the farming sector, such a foreign industry to me at the time, would eventually consume my life and would have me swapping my stilettos for muddy boots, permanently. I'll forever be grateful for that slow news day.

After I'd interviewed him, Sam asked me for my business card claiming he 'wanted a copy of the story', but I saw his cheeky smile and caught his flirtatious gaze. As it turned out, there was much more in store for the two of us than the half-baked story about meat consumption that we'd conjured up together in an effort to fill my evening news bulletin. When I got back to the office that afternoon, Sam had emailed me and asked me where he could get a good steak while he was in town. I'm pretty sure I rolled my eyes as I typed 'Literally, anywhere. Rockhampton is the beef capital!' We emailed back and forth a few more times before he asked me out for a friendly drink over the weekend before he left town. So on Sunday, 8 December 2013, full of curiosity and hungover as hell after a night out with friends, I dragged myself to the pub to meet this smooth-talking country man. A casual afternoon drink turned into a seven-hour-long catch-up that neither of us saw coming, followed by an incredible dinner and endless conversation. As the restaurant started closing up for the night and we prepared to part ways, I realised I didn't want the night to end and I knew Sam felt the same. I was intrigued by him and felt deeply connected despite the fact I'd not even so much as kissed the man. When he hopped in a cab and headed back to his hotel after we said our goodbyes, I felt a pang of sadness in the pit of my stomach. I liked this guy a lot. And although I'd sworn off men at the time, having had my heart broken into a million pieces in my early twenties, I just couldn't shake the feeling that we were destined to meet again. And sometimes destiny needs a little nudge. Luckily Sam isn't shy.

A couple of weeks later, I did the unthinkable. After several long phone calls and some flirty texts, I agreed to hop on a plane and meet Sam for a weekend in Brisbane. Anyone who knows me well enough knows that I'm not the type of girl to head off and spend two nights in a hotel with a random man I'd met only once—without at least doing a police check first and perhaps getting a PI to tail him in the meantime to suss out any red flags or skeletons in his closet—but I did. I stepped off the plane in Brisbane to see Sam waiting for me at the gate and in that moment, I knew that whatever this was, whoever he was, I wanted him. Sam, ever the gentleman, offered to book separate hotel rooms for us for the duration of our stay. It's safe to say we never booked that second room.

A whirlwind long-distance romance followed our weekend together and Sam and I got very serious, very quickly. He even temporarily moved up to the Rockhampton region to work on a nearby farm two hours away to be closer to me. I lived for Friday nights, counting down the hours until I'd hear his ute pull up at my apartment, marking the start of our weekend together. In mid-2014, I finally got my big break with Channel Nine and was offered a job with *A Current Affair* in Brisbane. I immediately resigned from my Rockhampton role with Channel Seven started packing and a few weeks later jumped into my little blue Honda Jazz to make the eight-hour trip south. Sam took a big leap of faith by moving to the big smoke to be with me and we've been inseparable since that day. For the next five years, we travelled around the country together for our respective careers. I was busy grinding it out in TV while Sam dusted off his suit and tie and forged a successful career in the corporate agribusiness world. However, it wasn't long before the glamour of our media and corporate jobs wore off, and my country boy and I were getting itchy feet.

It was by the pool at a resort in Thailand while on our honeymoon in late 2017 that Sam and I first crafted the idea of creating a beef business and moving back to his home state of Tassie. I knew that Sam yearned to move back to the land and, despite being born and raised in the city, I had been depleted by metropolitan living. I'd had enough of the stresses of the corporate world and the rat race, and I was ready for something new that would breathe life back into me. There was something so romantic and enticing about swapping the city for the country, so when Sam first broached the idea of buying our own farm I didn't need any convincing. After all, I'd watched enough episodes of *Farmer Wants a Wife*—life on the land looked so idyllic and relaxing and the thought of running our own business together on a farm seemed incredibly liberating.

I should add—minor detail—that before our big country move, we were living and working in Melbourne and had recently welcomed our son Elliot into the world. And while I'd spent my career fearlessly confronting criminals and chasing conman after conman, those encounters had nothing on the challenges I faced as a new mum. In the early months, I spent many hours on the bathroom floor sobbing as I struggled to connect with my inconsolable, colicky newborn. The sleep deprivation I experienced with a baby who woke up every 45 minutes throughout the night was excruciating, and the initial impact on my relationship with my husband was heart-wrenching as we shifted from a spontaneous, madly-in-love couple to two exhausted people passing each other like ships in the night. I didn't enjoy the early weeks and months of motherhood and I'm not afraid to admit that. I felt alone, I felt confined—despite living in a big city—and I honestly thought that I'd ruined my life. I have no doubt that I suffered from postnatal depression as well as what I like to call 'postnatal shock'. For my entire life, I'd been in control. I was in the driver's seat when it came to my career, and that in many ways had shaped my identity. But when I became a mother, I lost control. I was untethered. I have spent the past four years trying to find myself again, and I credit our country move with enabling me to do that.

> We shifted from a spontaneous, madly-in-love couple to two exhausted people passing each other like ships in the night.

So, farm life and the picturesque setting of rural Tasmania felt like my ticket out of hell, a fresh start in a completely new environment. However, I wasn't at all prepared for what awaited me.

In 2019, Sam and I boarded *Spirit of Tasmania* with six-month-old Elliot in tow and made the trip across Bass Strait. Before arriving at our new farm, I had a firm idea in my mind of what being a rural mum would be like. I assumed it would be easier, that it would be a natural transition and that life and motherhood in the country would be less stressful than the day-to-day chaos of the city. I naively thought that being married to a farmer and working from home meant that Sam would be around all the time to be with me and help me with the kids. However, my romanticised, city-fuelled ideas of what being a mum on the land would be like were obliterated the moment I became one. To begin with, there was nothing romantic about it. It was an incredibly hard transition and I was navigating it alone as a new mum. I thought, if they say it takes a village to raise a child, then where the hell is mine?

I remember the first day on the farm, just Elliot and me. Sam was out working and I'd never felt so isolated. Overnight, I'd lost my village. I had lost access to my support network and to local services and resources. We had no family or friends here and Sam's closest relatives were a three-hour drive away. I could no longer take Elliot for a walk in the pram up the road to meet my Melbourne mothers' group for coffee, and I even needed to buy a new pram that would withstand the paddocks and the rocky, muddy terrain at our doorstep just so I could walk around the farm alone. I didn't know anyone in the area, there were no local mothers' groups, Uber Eats was a thing of the past and my career options were limited. This was certainly no episode of *Farmer Wants a Wife* and I felt ripped off! Where were the romantic dates with my husband, sitting on hay bales, sipping wine at sunset, enjoying our magnificent view? Instead, day and night, I was competing for Sam's attention with cattle, machinery and a growing list of farm jobs he just never seemed able to finish.

I tried to embrace our new rural life as best as I could as I sat alone at home with our baby boy, but at times I thought that we had made a huge mistake in moving to the farm and I was miserable for those first few months. I struggled mentally after having Elliot and these feelings only intensified when we moved to Tasmania—I just did a damn good job of hiding it from everyone, my husband included. I felt too guilty to share my struggles with Sam as he was incredibly busy and stressed building our business. He was rarely home and worked seven days a week because, as I quickly discovered, most farmers don't get to take weekends off. While the cattle were cute, I felt incredibly frustrated that they still needed feeding, moving and checking on a Saturday and Sunday too (how dare they!).

As weeks turned into months, the sinking feeling of loneliness in the pit of my stomach just wouldn't go away. I finally realised that deep down what I really yearned for was to connect with other rural mums. I wanted to know that, despite how isolated I felt, I wasn't alone, that I wasn't failing and that some of the challenges I was facing as a mum on the land were understandable. I searched online, scoured social media, browsed parenting podcasts and soon realised that what I desperately needed didn't exist. I wanted a platform dedicated to telling the stories of rural mothers: a platform that would celebrate us, connect us and tell our tales of trials and tribulations raising kids in rural Australia. Suddenly, I realised what I had to do.

And that's where the idea for Motherland was born.

> I wanted to know that, despite how isolated I felt, I wasn't alone . . .

Motherland began as a podcast that I started from our dining-room table on the farm. It shares the incredible stories of rural mums: real, raw and powerful tales of motherhood told by women living on the land. Through their extraordinary grit, strength and capabilities, these women are dismantling the typical 'farmer's wife' stereotype, one story at a time. All these women are mothers, and some are also farmers, employees or entrepreneurs who are redefining life in the bush and mothering on the land. In many ways, these women lead vastly different lives but we are all bonded together by the unique challenges and opportunities of being rural mums.

For some of us, the geographical and social isolation is crippling; for others, it's access to adequate medical care for themselves and their family that they struggle with most. Childcare options are limited in many rural communities; the nearest town or hospital can be hours away and local postnatal support non-existent. It's not uncommon for rural kids to be homeschooled and, of course, for a lot of families the grocery run is a very planned weekly, fortnightly or even monthly road trip, so you don't want to forget the milk!

But whether you live in remote outback Australia or smack bang in the middle of a tiny country town, when you partner up with or marry a rural man, there's no doubt that you marry the land too. Like many rural dads, Sam was back at work 24 hours after our second child Evie was born and I cried almost every day when he walked out the door to work. Paternity leave, let alone annual leave, is a luxury many rural families can only dream of, and it's hard not to feel resentful at times. So yes, it can be difficult and lonely here, but mostly, for me at least, life feels full and free. My perceptions of motherhood have completely changed since moving to the land—being socially isolated and disconnected from others has highlighted to me that in so many ways we are doing this parenting thing all wrong.

We were never meant to mother alone. We need a village and we used to have one. Since the dawn of time, mothers in communities across the globe have raised their children together; they bathed their children together in rivers, shared stories and leaned on their elders for guidance. Village life fostered a sense of togetherness, and the responsibilities of raising a child didn't fall solely on the nuclear family unit (mum and dad)—it literally took a village. But sadly, in most western societies today, we parent in such an individualistic culture. The pressure and impacts of this are particularly evident in rural communities where mums (and dads) are more isolated and less likely to have that physical village to support them.

Over the past few years it has become abundantly clear to me that women, and especially mothers, are the backbone of rural communities and rural industries across our country. They are the glue that holds households together and they take on much of the workload, including the emotional and physical labour that comes with raising children and that still, unfortunately and stereotypically, falls on us. But regardless of whether we thrive in this role or are simply trying to survive while wearing all the hats, life on the land is uniquely different for everyone and we need to do more to support the incredible work rural women do. What has been most exciting to experience firsthand is the strong sense of camaraderie within the rural motherhood community. I've harnessed the power of a virtual village of rural mums to support me through some of my toughest times, and there's no doubt that social media has enabled me to form meaningful, long-distance friendships with women across Australia who have been a lifeline for me when I have needed it most.

In between having Elliot and Evie, I suffered a devastating miscarriage. The physical ordeal lasted for two weeks but the emotional toll lasted much longer and reared its ugly head at random moments over the following months. It is still painful to think about. The day I found out that we would never meet this baby, I had driven into town, had a haircut then skipped to a routine ultrasound only to be told there was no heartbeat. Terrified of being put under a general anaesthetic and going into surgery, I opted to let nature take its course. It wasn't until eight days later, on Christmas Eve, that my body finally let that pregnancy go. The pain was excruciating. It felt like I was in labour and I suppose, in a way, I was. The next day, Christmas Day, while still bleeding, I hopped on the quad bike with Sam and Elliot and did a few jobs around the farm. Looking back now, I realise I didn't process that loss in the way I should have and needed to. At the time, I just 'got on with it', an attitude that I have carried with me since we moved here. The world 'resilient' is thrown around a lot to describe farmers and country people and I'll admit that I have felt the need to be 'tough' out here, perhaps, subconsciously, to prove that I'm not a fragile city princess. But growing Motherland and pushing rural women to go deep and be vulnerable through sharing their own stories has shown me that I can be more honest with myself about my own story.

As an example, talking about my miscarriage with other farming mums really helped. And then later, when the anxiety I experienced throughout my pregnancy with Evie crippled me, I had an entire network of rural women to support me. Looking back, I really didn't connect with Evie until she was physically in my arms, alive. I was so petrified of losing her. But when she was here and I faced motherhood 2.0, I leaned into the Motherland community and I haven't stopped leaning on them since. Connecting with other rural mums has helped pull me out of my mental slumps; sharing some of their darkest moments as well as their highest highs has been a profoundly beautiful privilege that I know has helped rural mums feel less alone.

But for all the challenges that many rural mums face, there is so much joy and freedom. We live a highly addictive lifestyle that most, me included, would not swap for anything. I believe rural mothers are some of the most undervalued and under-celebrated women in this country; their stories are diverse and inspiring. And now, some of these ordinary rural women, with extraordinary stories of motherhood, have a platform. Motherland has taken me and my listeners from the top of the Territory to the southern tip of Tassie. Over the past three-and-a-half years, I've interviewed more than 200 rural mothers and the opportunity to capture some of their stories in writing feels like a pivotal moment for rural mums everywhere.

So, before I introduce you to fourteen inspirational rural mothers, I would like to say a special thankyou to the entire Motherland community. As Motherland has grown, so have I. The rural women I have connected with over the past few years have made me a better mum, a better partner, a better businesswoman and a better me. They have opened my eyes to the possibilities of this incredible rural life we are lucky to live and have made each of my challenges as a mum—every phase and every struggle—less isolating. Not only have I survived but I have *thrived* on the land since I started sharing their stories, because these women have been my lifeline and my village.

As Motherland has grown, so have I. The rural women I have connected with over the past few years have made me a better mum, a better partner, a better businesswoman and a better me.

Through their unwavering honesty and camaraderie, they have made me feel at home on the land. And what an incredible home it is.

# 1

# Karen Brock: Nowhere to run

## Meander Valley, Tasmania

Karen Brock still vividly remembers the gut-wrenching fear she felt as her bedroom door started cracking around her. She was sitting on the floor with her back pressed against the door, trying to prevent her abusive husband from storming in from the other side. But she knew there was no stopping him when he went into one of these fits of rage and his adrenaline was peaking. Desperate to escape, Karen scoured the room, searching for something she could throw at the window to shatter it. But there was nothing. And what was the point? Her husband had destroyed their home phone moments earlier, so she had no way of calling for help. And where would she run to? Karen lived on a dairy farm in rural Tasmania with two young children: there was nowhere to go and no one to hear her scream.

'You are isolated, you are in the middle of a paddock with kilometres of paddocks around that and there's no help.'

Karen's home with the man she loved was supposed to be her haven, but it wasn't long before it quickly turned into her hell. The marriage lasted five years and Karen was the target of physical and emotional abuse throughout that period. She was regularly beaten, raped and mentally traumatised, and agonisingly she had more than just her own wellbeing to think about. At the height of the violence she endured, her son was five years old and her daughter was just three. And while her now ex-husband Paul (not his real name) never physically hurt the children, sadly, they were regular witnesses to the violence that enveloped their family home. While Karen knew she had to find a way out, she felt incredibly isolated, and not just geographically.

You are isolated, you are in the middle of a paddock with kilometres of paddocks around that and there's no help.

More than 30 years on from the events of that night, Karen was sitting at my dining-room table while I recorded her story.

As an experienced journalist, I'm usually prepared for my interviews, but this one absolutely floored me. I invited Karen onto the *Motherland* podcast after she was announced as Tasmania's AgriFutures Rural Woman of the Year in 2020. I'd planned on asking her about her career as a specialist in plant tissue culture delivering improvements to the food production sector. I figured I'd have to find a way to weave in her motherhood journey and would simply ask how she juggled it all and poke and prod to see if there were any stand-out memories from her life over the years. I had absolutely no idea about Karen's devastating experience with domestic violence until she bravely opened up and began sharing it with me. I also didn't realise until after we had spoken that this very intimate conversation with me was the first time Karen had spoken publicly about what happened to her. It was a privilege to provide her with the platform to do so, and it warms me to say that we've stayed connected since.

Karen grew up in a strict, Christian household on a farm in Tasmania's Meander Valley. She adored horses, so she was incredibly excited when her parents bought her one when she was ten years old. However, it came with conditions and those conditions were that she had to work that horse regularly and help muster her father's cows and sheep. Karen recalls heading up to the Western Tiers mountains on horseback in freezing conditions. She describes it as 'bastard weather' that would come in as half snow, half rain, with the wind so fierce it felt like it was cutting her skin. As a young girl, Karen would be huddled over on her horse bringing home thousands of sheep in the sleet. While it was tough at times, she absolutely loved her life on the land. She was taught at a very young age to work hard, but she made sure she played hard too.

'My gosh, I was always free, the freedom was just incredible. I'd get on the horse and my brother and I would head off and we wouldn't come home until dark. There were no mobile phones, we'd be exploring—we were the pioneers of Meander! We had everything and we never felt any fear.'

While Karen enjoyed immense freedom throughout her childhood on the family farm, there were certain expectations she was under pressure to live up to. Her parents sent her to a private school and made it very clear that by investing in her education they expected that she would leave the cattle work and sheep work behind, forge a career outside the farm gate and work her way up to leadership and management roles. In fact, while many rural parents are quite happy for their children to partner up with other 'rurals', Karen's father stipulated that under no circumstances was she to marry a farmer. At the time, Karen couldn't understand why but, quite simply, her parents wanted her to expand her horizons and have a different life off the land. What happened next stunned everyone.

At eighteen, Karen rebelled and went against her family's wishes. She found a job working on a local dairy farm where she met and fell in love with a farmer named Paul. This rural romance added kerosene to an enormous fire that erupted within Karen's family, made worse when Karen unexpectedly fell pregnant at the tender age of nineteen. By that point, Karen's religious parents were so outraged that it wasn't long before they started to distance themselves from her all together. Karen soon felt a wave of shame wash over as she faced being ostracised from her own family and her local community for being an unmarried young mum.

'I felt like a failure, I felt terrible. I had my parents say to me, "We've just spent a shit tonne of money on your education so you didn't end up with a dairy farmer, and now look at you!"'

Karen had been taught her whole life that if you make your bed you have to lie in it, and this fuelled her feelings of isolation. Soon after discovering she was pregnant, she made the enormous and emotional decision to leave Tasmania to save her family the embarrassment of her unplanned pregnancy, and she followed Paul to the mainland, where he'd just been offered a job working on a dairy farm in regional Victoria. But instead of heading to Paul's new rural base straight away, Karen made a heartbreaking detour. She had decided the best thing for everyone was to put her baby up for adoption, such was the intensity of her shame. After doing some research on the adoption process and a few months into her pregnancy, she flew to Sydney in search of work and a temporary home while she awaited the birth of the baby whom she planned to give up. Karen admits that at the time she felt disconnected from her unborn child and overwhelmed by the weight on her shoulders—a young mum with no income and little support. When she arrived in Sydney, she had no money, no plan and just a suitcase of clothes to her name. She sought shelter at a women's refuge in the city's east and lived there for several months. She eventually found a job babysitting for a local family and was able to start earning money and preparing for the arrival of her son and the adoption paperwork that would follow.

Karen gave birth to a baby boy she named Chaise, and the days that followed were a blur. As she lay in hospital feeding him and bonding with him, her plans to put him up for adoption went out the window very quickly. She was consumed with love for her newborn son and knew that no matter how difficult her circumstances, or how great the shame, she could never give him up. Together, they moved to regional Victoria to reunite with Paul and give family life on the farm a real go together. Karen moved there full of love and hope for the three of them, but the dreams she had for her new family were slowly shattered as cracks began to form in her relationship with Paul. Karen says that, looking back now, there were several early warning signs of toxic behaviour from the man she loved, but she was young and naive and never imagined that he would become violent.

Not long after Karen and baby Chaise joined Paul, some troubling behaviour soon escalated into domestic abuse that shook Karen to her core. Initially, Paul's rage wasn't directed at Karen at all; the first real and very frightening red flag was when their pet cat scratched Chaise. This marked the beginning of a horrific few years at home for Karen.

'I came home one day and Paul was running around the house with a gun chasing the cat. He hurled the cat at the wall and then shot it dead in the middle of our living room.

'Then he just walked outside as if nothing had happened.'

Shaking from shock, Karen was left to clean up the mess and bury their pet cat. In those moments she realised that the man she had fallen in love with had a terrifying alter ego; but she still had no idea just how terrifying things would get. A year later, Karen and Paul moved back to their home state of Tasmania, got married and focused on settling down and setting up their own farming operation. The toxicity of their relationship was growing and it wasn't long before Karen's home life began to crumble around her. Paul started lashing out more and more; soon Karen was the target of verbal and emotional abuse that escalated into physical violence and assault.

I asked Karen to tell me about the first time Paul hit her. For the most part, she had blocked out that first assault—it was a traumatic experience that left her reeling from shock. But she remembers that the two of them were in the dairy bickering about something insignificant when suddenly Paul snapped and started punching her. After the attack, he apologised. Bruised and battered, Karen simply shut down from the pure shock of it all. Once she had time to digest what had happened, Paul became remorseful and she wrongly assumed that the violence directed at her was a one-off. But it wasn't. The abuse she endured for the next few years was relentless.

'From there, I had to fight. I was a warrior woman. Everyone has a warrior inside their heart but sometimes they are just too scared to unleash it.'

Karen fell pregnant with their daughter when Chaise was just a year old. It was at that point that she started thinking seriously about how she could leave her abusive husband, but her options were limited. She was living on a farm; she was isolated from any resources and services that could help really her and she was financially dependent on her husband. With two young children to raise, she knew that if she left she had to have some form of financial independence so she could support herself and her kids. So humbly and quietly but very determinedly, Karen enrolled herself in a horticulture course through TAFE, where she hoped to carve out some sort of career in the agricultural industry. A few months later, she travelled interstate to the Melbourne Flower Show for a couple of days and fell head over heels for the cut flower industry. It was love at first sight and from that trip onwards Karen was fixated on how she could create a career in the flower industry and use it as her ticket out of the nightmare at home.

To Karen's surprise, she inherited $25,000 when her grandmother passed away, and she tried to keep it a secret for as long as possible. She knew that if Paul found out, he'd do what he could to take the money for himself and spend it on whatever he wanted for the farm. But, despite Karen's best efforts, it wasn't long before the secret was out. She'd had the money set up under her name in a private bank account that Paul didn't have access to. However, when the local bank manager called the house one day to chat with Karen about her account, unfortunately it was Paul who answered the phone. The employee made a passing comment that indicated he needed to talk to Karen about an account that only she was authorised to discuss, and this information sent Paul off the rails.

'I got the belting of my life after that. But I refused to give up that money because it was my lifeline.'

Karen suffered another year of brutal physical and sexual assaults before she mustered up the courage to tell Paul that their relationship was over and she wanted out. It was a strategic move that she had planned carefully, because by that point she had the TAFE course under her belt and qualifications that would lead to job security. She knew that she was finally able to get herself and her children away from the violence. For Karen, the last straw came one day when, following a disagreement on the drive home, Paul punched her as she stepped out of their car when they'd reached the farm. Karen snapped.

'I turned to him, and I said "That is the last time you're ever going to do that. Get out and don't come home." But he did come home.'

Karen's desperate words fell on deaf ears. Paul left the farm for a few hours but came home that night angrier than ever. What Karen endured next is horrific. She'd been hiding in their bedroom pressed against the door, desperately trying to keep the door shut, but he stormed his way in and the violent attack lasted several minutes. As a result of that assault—which would be the last time Paul ever laid a hand on her—Karen was left with broken ribs, corked arms and thighs and a bruised neck where he'd strangled her. After the attack was over, Paul left and Karen stumbled into the hallway, falling to her knees.

'I really didn't think I was going to get out of that room. I remember when he drove out, I just sat down in the hall, relieved that he had left my aura. And my five-year-old came out of the bedroom and put his arms around me and said, "It's all over now, Mummy. He's gone." That just broke me.'

Karen drove straight to town the next day to see her doctor and to report the assault. It was the first time she'd told anyone about the domestic violence she'd been suffering all those years and it took a lot of courage to do so. Living in a small, rural community can make it especially hard for victims of domestic violence to seek help, and not just because of a lack of services but because of a lack of anonymity. When you live in the country, word travels fast and sometimes it feels like nothing is private. Gossip spreads like wildfire, and it's common to feel that even your most personal information isn't safe at all. For many rural women, there is often a fear of the stigma and shame linked to domestic violence, as well as a lack of transport options when it comes to trying to escape a situation. In addition, the local police, doctors and social workers often know both parties involved, which can make it especially difficult to speak up, let alone leave. The sad reality is that it's difficult to ascertain accurate rates of domestic violence in rural communities because many victims simply do not report it. However, what we do know is that women living in regional, rural and remote communities are more likely to be hospitalised as a result of family and domestic violence than those living in major cities. For countless women, Karen included, wanting to leave is one thing but escaping is another thing altogether.

> My five-year-old said, 'It's all over now, Mummy. He's gone.' That just broke me.

Thankfully, Karen not only wanted to escape but she had a plan. When she saw her doctor that day, she stripped off her clothes and asked him to document and take photos of every single mark on her body, from her broken ribs to the bruises and strangulation marks. The doctor, who'd known Karen since she was a little girl, was horrified and he urged her to go to the police immediately to lay charges.

'I said no. I said, "That man has just lost his family. He's an incredibly angry person right now. It will wear off eventually, but he's lost control, and if I go to the police, I'm going to be in even more danger than I'm in now."'

Karen did go to see a solicitor that day and successfully filed for a twelve-month apprehended violence order (AVO) against her husband. But it wasn't worth the paper it was written on, because, even though by law her husband was banned from setting foot their farm, that didn't stop him from coming back. While Karen never saw him, he left threatening messages that sent a signal to Karen that he had been there and he could still get to her. Karen changed all the locks, but Paul broke into her home one day when she was out. She came home that night to find that a pair of farming overalls that she'd repaired and sewn back together had been cut with scissors from the crotch to the hem at the bottom of one leg. Nothing else in the house was touched. It sent shivers up Karen's spine.

'That's when you go, "Shit. I'm sitting in the middle of God knows how many acres and my house has been violated, despite the fact that I've got an AVO which clearly means nothing."'

That night Karen realised that as long as she remained on the farm she would never truly be safe and Paul would always have power over her. After that incident, Karen and her children packed up their belongings and moved into another farmhouse on a nearby property—and this time, Karen put some safety precautions in place. She got creative, rigging up her new driveway with sensor lights on a timer connected to a basketball siren that echoed loudly across the valley when anyone tried to approach the house in a car. Thankfully, Paul never breached the AVO again, and twelve months later Karen filed for divorce. He didn't object. Karen was finally free.

In spite of all she's been through, Karen refuses to be classified as a 'victim', and if you met her it wouldn't take you long to realise that such a label does not describe her. Of all the rural mums I've had the honour of interviewing, Karen has been one of the few I've been lucky enough to meet in person. She is one of the most remarkable women I've ever known, not only because of what she's survived but also because of how she's thrived as a leader in the rural sector, undeterred by all she's endured in her personal life. Karen's story doesn't end with her escaping her abusive marriage and she hasn't let it define her. In fact, her life really began after she left Paul.

Karen had been working as a flower-packing manager at a large Tasmanian nursery at the time her divorce was settled.

Soon after it was finalised, she decided it was time to leave the small-town gossip behind, so she took her then four-year-old daughter and seven-year-old son to Sydney where she was offered a big career break at the iconic Flemington Market near Homebush, working for one of the largest flower wholesalers in Australia. Karen and her kids lived in the big smoke for two years before Tassie came calling and she decided to move back home to further her career in the local flower industry.

Karen took on a managerial role at national flower wholesaler Tesselaar Flowers, which at the time was producing a patented range of nursery plants across Tasmania that were being sold locally and exported to the mainland. When the company wound up its Tasmanian operation a few years later, Karen was offered the opportunity to buy the nursery side of the business and that's when her Brocklands business was born. With limited capital but limitless grit and determination, Karen sold her car, got a loan and poured her life savings into buying the plants and stock and setting up her own nursery.

Since then, Karen has grown her Brocklands enterprise into a horticulture powerhouse. She started with 25 plant species and quickly grew her operation to more than 200 in just twelve months. She cut deals with the likes of Bunnings, supplying their stores across the state, all while working on bigger dreams in the background. Alongside her wholesale nursery, Karen now uses plant tissue culture science to produce more than one million genetically improved plants every year, with a focus on disease resistance, climate tolerance and high yields. She's created a process that delivers faster harvesting timeframes for farmers and as a result she is contributing immensely to future food security for the agriculture sector.

'I do actually have to pinch myself. Never let anyone say you can't do something, because the warrior woman is sitting in your heart.'

Finally, as my coffee catch-up with Karen draws to a close, I carefully ask her how she feels now about her ex-husband. Surprisingly, Karen says that she has left the anger and the hurt behind and, in many ways, has forgiven Paul. She adds that he has since sought professional help for his abusive behaviour and has worked hard to rebuild his life. Karen's children have a good relationship with their father now, and she has never stopped Paul from connecting with them. Their children are now adults, living lives of their own, having children of their own. While so much of their life as a family was broken in those early years, they have all worked hard to move past the trauma and pain. Karen even agreed to be in the same room as Paul a few years ago when they both celebrated their daughter's wedding.

I do actually have to pinch myself. Never let anyone say you can't do something, because the warrior woman is sitting in your heart.

Karen has now well and truly moved on from that dark time in her life and, while the scars remain, she says the wounds have healed. On a professional level, her career has flourished, going from strength to strength. Her personal life has transformed for the better too. After Karen's divorce all those years ago, when the pain and trauma of her abusive marriage were still raw, she put on a lot of weight, subconsciously believing that by making herself unattractive no man would want her and therefore no man would be able to hurt her again. While Karen tried to sabotage her chance of finding love and being happy again, fate had other plans—she met a man named Tim through work and this meeting changed everything.

Tim was sensitive and kind and soon fell madly in love with Karen. She opened up about what she'd been through in her first marriage and he listened. He was patient and respectful and the two of them grew closer as Karen leaned in to love, taking a chance and learning to trust again. In 2008, they were married and since then have lived on their farm in Tasmania's West Tamar region. They now run the Brocklands business together, side by side.

Karen is a trailblazing businesswoman, a doting mother and now a grandmother. She's also a motorbike enthusiast who loves nothing more than hitting the road on a weekend and feeling the cool Tassie wind in her hair. She is bubbly, loud and warm and her presence is instantly felt in any room she enters. I've had the pleasure of getting to know her more over the past couple of years since she first sat at my dining-room table and poured her heart out, hoping that by sharing her story, she would help other women. And she has. The strong, confident, capable and successful woman Karen has become is a world away from the scared young rural mum she used to be, the mum who was once told time and time again that she was worthless and that she would amount to nothing. Luckily, she didn't listen. Because boy is she something now.

# 2

# Julie McDonald: Life after loss

## Devoncourt Station, Queensland

Julie McDonald was standing in the middle of 240,000 hectares of farmland when in an instant, life changed forever, both for her and for her four daughters. Julie's husband, the love of her life, lay critically injured while she scrambled for her phone, desperate to call for help. But help was a very long way away, and Julie felt a deep pang of isolation when she realised all she could do was wait and hope.

'It was very traumatic. We were 30 kilometres from the homestead and it was the most terrifying moment of my life,' she says.

While Julie's story is one of immense pain and loss, it's also one of incredible love for the grazier she fell for, the beautiful family they created and her unwavering connection to the

Australian outback, a connection that began sixteen years before that fateful day.

Julie grew up on a 40-hectare hobby farm on the outskirts of the quiet town of Cudal near Orange in central west New South Wales. She had an idyllic childhood with her three siblings and loved spending time both at home and with her grandparents, who owned a property nearby. Julie's family was heavily involved in the local community, and she enjoyed everything from pony club to swimming club and ballet. She went to primary school locally before she was given the opportunity to spread her wings and head to the big smoke to continue her education through high school.

At age twelve, like many rural kids, Julie left home and moved to Sydney to attend boarding school. After finishing school, she opted to stay in the city and attend university, where she studied accounting and finance, enjoying the life of a university student and all the excitement the city had to offer.

By the time Julie graduated she had spent almost a decade in Sydney and, while she loved her time in the city, she had absolutely no plans to carve out a career there. Country life was in her bones, it was home, and she made plans to return to the region of her childhood—but she had no idea that soon she would find herself in some of the most remote, far-flung parts of the country, places that would make Orange feel like New York City in comparison.

When Julie returned home, she locked in a job working as a tax accountant, which she enjoyed. But after a couple of years, she started to get itchy feet and decided it was time to throw caution to the wind and see more of the world beyond her own backyard. In 1996, she headed overseas on a backpacking adventure across Europe—exploring, partying and soaking in foreign cultures, a world away from the Australian countryside. After six months, with her funds low but her spirits high, she decided it was time to come home, feeling ready to settle into her profession—or so she thought. Julie moved back to Orange and got stuck into her former job as an accountant. But a few months later, she was craving more adventure. Fortuitously, one of her girlfriends invited her to join her on a trip to northern Australia and, much to her parent's bemusement, Julie packed her bags again—only this time no one realised that she'd be leaving home for good.

'My friend was offered a teaching job at Mount Isa and asked me to come with her, and I just said yes! I was ready for the next adventure and didn't know what that looked like, but knew I had some business skills that I could use across the country so I'd find work somewhere.'

Three months after landing in Queensland's Gulf country, Julie and her friend had settled into Mount Isa life. They both worked hard in their respective jobs (Julie finding a job at a local accounting firm) while soaking in the social scene of the far north. It was during one of their social outings to a nearby town that Julie's life changed forever.

It was a crisp June evening in 1997 when a carefree and footloose Julie caught the eye of a handsome local cattleman standing at the bar of Cloncurry's iconic Post Office Hotel. It was a significant few days on the region's social calendar, with the town's annual show about to kick off the next day and thousands of people flocking to the town to celebrate.

'I had absolutely no idea who he was or what he did when we met.'

A mutual friend introduced the pair while they were having a drink at the bar and a casual chat soon turned into endless conversation, dancing and flirting. Little did Julie know what awaited her after this chance meeting with eligible bachelor Alexander McDonald, affectionately known as 'Zanda'—who would become one of Australia's most prominent and influential graziers.

'With all the noise and music, I didn't catch his name properly, so I was calling him "Zando" for a while, which ended up being a running joke between us over the years!'

When Zanda met Julie, he was more interested in hearing about her life than sharing details of his own. He bombarded her with questions, eager to learn more about the smart, warm and savvy woman who'd landed in this neck of the woods. He didn't talk about himself, opting not to mention that his family was one of the largest private landholders in the world, with properties covering some 3.36 million hectares of Queensland and with a rich history steeped in Australian agriculture.

'True to his nature, that's how he lived his life. He was a really curious and humble man and was always more interested in knowing what was going on around him than talking about himself,' says Julie.

> I had absolutely no idea who he was or what he did when we met.

As the night and festivities started to wind down and the temperature dropped, Julie was getting cold, so Zanda lent her his jumper before walking her back to her hotel. As they said their goodbyes, Julie knew deep down that they would see each other again, firstly because she had a jumper to return but mostly because it just felt right and they were drawn to each other. True to her instinct, that evening was just the beginning of their love story. Julie returned Zanda's jumper a week later, when Zanda travelled 200 kilometres to Mount Isa to see her. The rest, they say, is history. The pair fell hard and fast for each other over the following months; it was clear they'd both found the one.

While romance blossomed, for the first twelve months of their relationship Julie was busy working at an accounting firm in Mount Isa, and Zanda was 200 kilometres away at Devoncourt Station. It was fortuitous to have this time living relatively close to each other, as he was soon to move north to Rutland Plains Station, adding some 800 kilometres to the journey to see each other. Rutland Plains is one of his family's properties, made up of 223,000 hectares of cattle country, endless wetlands and spectacular wildlife in remote Cape York. While the pair lived worlds apart for that time, no distance could keep them from each other. Julie revelled in their whirlwind, long-distance romance, which included many trips to the station, where Zanda showed her his outback home from the air by helicopter. The vast landscape was at the same time breathtakingly beautiful and rugged. With their relationship forging strongly ahead, Julie soon had a big decision to make: was she ready to commit to a life in the remote outback? Without question, she was.

Zanda proposed to Julie on a rare weekend away in Cairns a year after they met. The proposal was as down-to-earth, spontaneous and humble, just like Zanda. He'd found a little brass curtain ring then got down on one knee, presenting it to Julie and asking her to marry him. Of course, Julie said yes and proudly wore the curtain ring until they picked out a formal engagement ring together.

'He just had a zest for life and an attitude of giving everything a go. I was on an adventure myself and I was just all-in with him.'

While Julie was all-in, she didn't really know exactly what she was in for, not moving in with Zanda at Rutland Plains Station until after the two of them were married. While rural life wasn't foreign to Julie, the remoteness of her new full-time address did come with some challenges.

'I can tell you, it was a real sink-or-swim scenario for me at times, and I had a lot of firsts. I learned a lot, very quickly.'

Julie quickly adapted to her new life in the bush and experienced things she'd never seen or done before. Saltwater crocodiles lurked in every waterhole and snakes were found both outside and inside their home. For up to five months of the year, during and following a good wet season, their roads were cut off, and through these times Julie and Zanda travelled everywhere by chopper and light aircraft, both piloted by Zanda. The property generated its own power by day, but they didn't have any electricity at night, so after dark everything was done by torchlight. Julie recalls these experiences not with complaint but with warm recollection. She and Zanda were a team, and under his guidance Julie quickly learned to chip in wherever she could, helping with everything from fencing to yard building across the vast landscape that surrounded them.

Nine months after moving to the station, Julie fell pregnant with their first daughter, Bella. Preparing for motherhood was a mission in itself, given how remote they were from a hospital. For all four of her pregnancies, Julie had to leave the station, leave Zanda and travel all the way to Brisbane, where she'd stay for the final weeks of her pregnancies, preparing for birth. This uprooting from home can be a jarring journey both physically and emotionally for many rural women across Australia who have to travel long distances to access the maternity services they need. At a time when many mums-to-be are home 'nesting', preparing for the imminent arrival of our bundle of joy, setting up the nursery and focusing on how to install the baby seat in the car, many rural women are pulled away from their safe haven and must venture to another town or to the city to give birth.

'The flying doctors don't like you to be up there and so remote right through to the end of your pregnancy, so you need to find somewhere to go and wait for the last four weeks.'

It doesn't seem like a big deal to Julie when she talks about it but it amazes me that for each of her four pregnancies, she had to pack up her things and move away from home for several weeks. Zanda was busy mustering for those final few weeks before their first-born, Bella, arrived, but he made the dash to Brisbane just in time and thankfully arrived the day she was born—a very special day, because she was born on his birthday. After a short stay in hospital, Julie headed back to the station, and she admits that she was a little unprepared for what motherhood had in store for her on the land.

> The flying doctors don't like you to be up there and so remote right through to the end of your pregnancy, so you need to find somewhere to go and wait for the last four weeks.

'I went back to the station thinking life's changed but it's not really going to change what I do. And I learned pretty quickly, and the hard way, that you can't just do everything you were doing with a tiny newborn in tow.'

But undeterred by a quickly growing family, welcoming four daughters in just five-and-a-half years, Julie was resolved to keep her feet firmly out on the station when she could. She ensured her little girl tribe tagged along for the ride whenever possible, spending time with Julie while she drove across the station checking water bores or dropping off lick blocks for the cattle. Life in the outback made for some testing parenting times at home too, especially when it came to something as simple as putting their little girls to bed.

'For our years at Rutland Plains, we had what is called a meat-safe cot, which has a timber frame surrounded by gauze to keep the mozzies and snakes away because our house wasn't snake-proof.'

Despite the challenges, Julie thrived as a mum on the station. Eighteen months after Bella was born, Zanda and she welcomed little Katie into the world. Not long after that, Zanda began taking over more and more responsibility for the growing family business further south, so he and Julie left Cape York and moved 1000 kilometres to Devoncourt Station near Cloncurry, the station where Zanda was raised. Over the next two years, Julie and Zanda welcomed two more daughters, Laura and Millie, and their family of six finally felt complete. The nearest school was 75 kilometres away, so Julie and Zanda decided to seek the support of a governess who helped guide their girls through School of the Air, their distance education taking place in a purpose-built schoolroom on the station.

Life was certainly busy for Julie and Zanda but their hearts were full. Julie spent most days in and out of both the office and the schoolroom, supporting the girls throughout their homeschooling education, while establishing herself in the McDonald family business, overseeing the office and administration staff. Increasingly, Zanda was pulled away from the station and his family, travelling across the world to Asia, Russia and Dubai, marketing their boxed beef and selling it to a growing number of overseas buyers. Zanda was also heavily involved with various CSIRO (Commonwealth Scientific and Industrial Research Organisation) projects and innovative trials across several properties—something he loved sinking his teeth into. He was fast becoming a highly respected public figure in the agriculture industry, while Julie was proving that she had the skills to support the family's cattle empire through its next stage of growth.

For the first few years as they reared their young tribe of four girls, Julie did a lot of solo parenting while Zanda was pulled away for work. But when he was home, he was present in all senses of the word. Julie warmly recalls how the girls would gather around him each night while he read books to them and how, outside on the station, he taught them many life skills, including teaching the eldest two girls how to drive. He'd take them out in his ute onto their airstrip, which provided a wide, open, safe space, free from cars and the perfect training ground for their first taste in the driver's seat. The girls grabbed every opportunity to go out and help their dad on the station, and he ensured they were well equipped with the basic skills for station life. He taught them how to fix things around the property, giving them each a set of pliers, and he would regularly take them out to do routine maintenance jobs together.

On the afternoon of Saturday, 16 March 2013, Zanda and Julie and three of the girls, Katie, Laura and Millie, headed out for some weekend work on the station together. Bella, the eldest sister, was away at boarding school at the time. A windmill on the station needed servicing, a regular job that Zanda would do several times a year.

Julie and the girls were working at ground level as Zanda worked above them. He had climbed up onto the lower platform of the windmill to tighten the bore casing when suddenly the tool slipped in his hands, causing him to lose his footing. He didn't have a chance to brace himself and fell four metres to the ground. It was a freak accident. After registering what had just happened, it took Julie a few moments to realise how serious the situation was. Zanda very clearly wasn't getting up and was in a lot of pain. As she desperately grabbed her phone to call for help, Julie was deeply aware that help was not going to arrive immediately.

'I had my mobile phone with me, which thankfully had a little bit of service, and I was able to call for help. But help didn't arrive for another hour.'

After calling emergency services, Julie nursed her husband and tried to keep her girls busy, sending them to scout for any dust on the horizon that would signal the arrival of the medical team. Julie also called Zanda's parents, who arrived before the Cloncurry Ambulance Service. Not long after the arrival of the ambulance, Lifeflight landed their helicopter at the scene. Zanda was airlifted to Mount Isa Hospital, then later transferred by the Royal Flying Doctor Service to the intensive care unit at Townsville Hospital. Julie says she knew at the time that Zanda's injuries were very serious, but she'd still been optimistic that he would pull through.

Heartbreakingly, after nineteen days in hospital, on 4 April 2013, Zanda passed away. His four daughters were aged twelve, eleven, nine and seven, and Julie faced the devastating task of breaking the news of their father's death to them. The shock and trauma of losing her husband was swiftly followed by the surreal realisation that she would now be raising her girls without him.

'I didn't have a lot of options to get counselling to deal with my grief because of where we live and the telephone just doesn't cut it. I did try to ring a helpline one night six weeks later. They asked me how long ago did he pass and I remember them saying it's "early days", and I just went, "Oh my God, this can't be early days; it just feels like a lifetime."'

While Julie grappled with her grief over the weeks and months that followed, she also desperately tried not to push her deepest fears onto her daughters. Zanda's death had rocked her to her core, particularly because it had been such a shock. Suddenly, the station seemed riddled with hazards. Whether the girls were out mustering on horseback or motorbikes, driving or slashing the airstrip, Julie struggled to shake her anxiety. She was determined to keep those worries to herself so her girls could continue living their life on the land fully and freely, as she knew they should, and just as Zanda would have wanted. Eventually, Julie was able to speak with a counsellor to help her deal with her own grief and better understand the process for her daughters' grief too. She felt responsible for helping the girls to grieve, and worried that they were not grieving the way she thought they should. But it soon became clear that she needed to step back and allow them each to process the heartache of losing their dad in their own way.

'That took an enormous weight off my shoulders because initially I wanted them all to grieve in a certain way. I felt this one wasn't crying enough, and this one wants this, and the littlest . . . What memories is she going to have of him? I would work myself up into knots about that.'

Almost 500 people from around Australia and overseas attended Zanda's funeral. Not only was he a much-loved son, husband and father, but he was a highly respected cattleman, known for his leadership and innovation. Zanda helped pioneer animal welfare practices across the sector, ensuring the family business was at the forefront of groundbreaking research and development, including the introduction of pain relief to improve welfare standards for castration, dehorning and branding. When Zanda died, every member of the McDonald family rallied to fill the gaping holes in the business, determined to work harder than ever to continue his work. Julie returned to work on the station two weeks after his death and stepped up to take on the role of chief financial officer. She moved into Zanda's office, opened up his emails and got to work, working hard to do what she could to continue the work he had been involved with across their business and the industry. The McDonald family, their business team and the wider agriculture sector have banded together to ensure Zanda's legacy lives on.

In 2014, the Platinum Primary Producers group, a collective of over 150 of Australia and New Zealand's top rural leaders, established an award in Zanda's name; the first winner was announced and awarded in 2015. The Zanda McDonald Award supports innovative young producers, turbocharging their career growth through a personalised mentoring and education program. The prestigious award has attracted some of agriculture's most talented future leaders and provides them with an impressive prize package. Julie says Zanda would be very humbled.

It's been ten years since Julie lost her husband and in that time she's nurtured her four girls through their next stages of life, from young girls to young women. Julie says she's had good days and bad days and has leaned on family, friends, industry colleagues and neighbours for support. She's a very strong and proud woman and admits that many times over the years she has had to swallow her pride and ask for help. When I ask her about the biggest challenge she's faced as a mum since she lost Zanda, her answer is heartbreakingly simple.

'The hardest part continues to be that I can't give them their father back. I know that sounds so obvious and probably silly but that is the thing that I struggle with the most.'

After immersing herself in work and motherhood over the past decade, the most recent chapter and challenge for Julie has been the prospect of an empty nest. All four of her girls have gone through boarding school, and Millie, her youngest, is seventeen, in her final year and the only one yet to graduate. The four sisters are all chasing big dreams and doing vastly different things. Bella has finished an international degree in classical music (cello), and plans to play in orchestras while she undertakes further study; Laura has enjoyed and worked her way through a gap year before heading to a New South Wales university to study animal science (genetics); and Katie has completed her agribusiness degree through the University of Queensland and is back at work at the grass roots level in a stock camp. The future is in good hands!

Julie continues to help lead the McDonalds' business as CFO while also making her own mark, working and investing more broadly in agriculture. She still calls Devoncourt Station home and adores the few times a year all her girls return for holidays. They're exceptionally handy young women too; if there's a fence to be fixed, out come the pliers and off they go. They have been raised to be incredibly strong and resourceful, a testament to the country upbringing they've had and to their incredible parents.

I can't give them their father back . . . that is the thing that I struggle with the most.

Julie says Zanda and she were the perfect match, and they would balance each other out in the best of ways. Zanda was a big thinker, not afraid to take a risk in business, while Julie has always been more risk averse. Together, they found their sweet spot. While Zanda is gone now and Julie will never stop missing him, he's still everywhere in her life in the most wonderful of ways. His innovative, adventurous, can-do attitude is Julie's daily inspiration, a reminder to take leaps of faith and push herself beyond what she thinks she is capable of.

'I used to ask myself what Zan would say or do in a particular situation, and that was often just the push I needed to jump in. I don't question myself quite so much anymore. Life is good, and I am surrounded by wonderful people and work in an industry I love. There are plenty of great things yet to come, for both me and our daughters, and for that I am so grateful.'

# 3

# Darrylin Gordon: Breaking the cycle

## Kimberley, Western Australia

In the heart of the remote and sparsely populated Kimberley region of Western Australia lies Lamboo Station. Owned by First Nations peoples and sitting on Jaru country, the property spans 360,000 hectares and is surrounded by hilly terrain and native bushland. Its red earth is home to proud Jaru woman Darrylin Gordon, whose family has lived on this land for generations. Lamboo and the surrounding region have a rich history that remained intact before white settlement, but when the first pastoralists arrived in the area in the early 1900s they divvied up the land that belonged to Darrylin's ancestors. Darrylin's grandfather Jabi was part of the Stolen Generation of Aboriginal and Torres Strait Islander children who were removed from their families between 1910 and 1970. Jabi was forcibly taken from his home when he was six years old and raised at a church mission. Though he was to become the most influential person in Darrylin's life, she didn't find out about his painful past until she was a teenager.

'It was very confronting to hear, and I had mixed emotions; I was angry. Jabi protected us a lot from his past.'

In the years that followed his release from the mission, Darrylin's granddad worked as a drover, moving cattle across the Kimberley and even as far as Queensland. After meeting Darrylin's grandmother at Halls Creek, 40 kilometres from Lamboo Station, the pair fell in love and went on to have ten children (I can't fathom this as I can't even cope with two!). They eventually settled down at Lamboo Station, where Darrylin's grandmother had grown up out bush, and Jabi got a job helping white settlers with the station work on the land that once belonged Aboriginal people, land that he never thought one day would be theirs again.

In 1994, the tables finally turned after a historic decision was made by the Western Australian government to return Lamboo Station to its traditional owners. The property was purchased by the now abolished Aboriginal and Torres Strait Islander Commission (ATSIC, 1990–2005), a government body set up by the Hawke government through which First Nations peoples were formally involved in the processes of government decisions affecting their lives. The property is now owned by the Ngunjiwirri Aboriginal Corporation, which was set up on behalf of the Jaru people by members of Darrylin's family. At the time, the government's main focus was simply to provide the Jaru people with land to live on, but since then it has become a commercial cattle enterprise and was, until recently, managed solely by the male members of Darrylin's family. However, almost 30 years after the historic decision to return the land to its traditional owners, Darrylin found herself fighting a different battle, one that had never been fought on that land before. She was desperate to break a deeply ingrained, intergenerational cycle that ran in her family, and in many others, both in Indigenous and non-Indigenous cultures.

'For generations, it's always been a man's job to run a farm. But I was born with this voice that said, "Well actually, that's BS and I don't believe that, because I have everything it takes."'

Darrylin gave me goosebumps as she explained with great passion that life on Lamboo is no longer a man's world. She has smashed every stereotype and glass ceiling on her way to the top as the first female manager in the station's history. She had to find a way to chase her dreams and also pay respect to her cultural heritage, while not conforming to the gender-based role most of her family expected from her. Darrylin and her ancestors have a deep connection to their land, something that is sacred to Darrylin. For the first few years of her life, Darrylin lived in the bush. And when I say in the bush, I don't mean that she lived in a farmhouse in the outback but rather, she'd spend each night cuddled up to her parents and sister and brother, camping under the stars. Immersed in her culture from an early age, she has also tried to break through some of its confines.

Throughout much of her childhood, Darrylin's father was a fencing contractor and his job meant that he and his family travelled across the Tanami Desert, working on various properties. Much of the region has since been declared a First Nations protected area or conservation zone and has various cultural sites scattered throughout. It is also home to several of Australia's rarest and most endangered animal species, including the bilby and the rufous hare wallaby. Darrylin and her family lived off the land over those early years, hunting kangaroos, turkeys and goannas, and foraging for other bush tucker such as bush plums and bush bananas.

'We didn't have running water or toilets for the first eight years. But we were so free, and we didn't feel like we missed out on anything. It taught us so many valuable life skills that we cherish.'

As a child, Darrylin soaked up like a sponge the wisdom and stories of her culture passed down from her elders. She'd regularly go walkabout with her grandparents, and they'd teach her about bush medicine, show her sacred cultural sites and burial sites, and explain more about the spirits of her ancestors that still roam the land. When the wet season came, they'd all move back to the old Lamboo homestead, where Darrylin's grandmother was tasked with teaching her about the domestic responsibilities that her culture expected of Darrylin as a young woman. Darrylin ensured she absorbed all those lessons and has always deeply respected her bloodline and her history. Yet as she grew older, she became insistent on carving out an entirely different future for herself, one that would see her step outside her culture's female mould.

As Darrylin entered her teens, she found the gender roles she had been taught to abide by increasingly frustrating. Traditionally, the role of First Nations women was to take on all domestic responsibilities, including cooking, cleaning and raising children, while the men were responsible for providing food, shelter and clothing. Those gender barriers and expectations continued to play out in modern working life on the cattle station. Darrylin found it extremely difficult to comprehend why she wasn't allowed to join the men and work out on the station, however much she yearned for it. By the time she hit puberty, Darrylin wasn't even allowed to be in the same workplace or space as her brothers when they were busy working with cattle and earning their living out on the property. Darrylin was expected to be home with the other females in her family, learning about the roles she was required to perform as a woman in her community.

'It was really frustrating for me, and I used to always ask my grandmother why? And say, "That's not fair."

'I just kept pushing the boundaries saying, look, I just don't want to do that, It's boring. I don't want to cook for my brothers, I'm not going to clean after them. I was very stubborn.'

Darrylin's stubbornness paid off but it took several years. She'd regularly get into trouble for taking off and running away from the house to find the boys who were out working on the station. She'd return home to find her grandmother waiting for her with a stick in hand and, after copping a brief hiding, she'd be sent off to do chores. Over the years, her beloved grandfather Jabi recognised that Darrylin's thirst for station life and farming was unquenchable. When she was twelve years old, he finally caved and allowed her to go out mustering with the boys for the first time. It was a big deal and sent a strong message to the rest of the men on the station, including her uncles, cousins and brothers. Not everyone was happy about it but Darrylin couldn't have cared less. She savoured every moment working on the station, ignoring the raised eyebrows and keeping up with the boys.

I just kept pushing the boundaries saying,
look, I just don't want to do that. It's boring.

At every possible opportunity during school holidays, Darrylin was on horseback helping the blokes with anything that got her hands dirty, from mustering cattle to drafting animals in the yards. Whether it was fencing or welding, you name it,

Darrylin was quick to learn and to get involved, and it wasn't long before she was giving the men a run for their money—she was more than keeping up. Little did they all know that one day Darrylin would be the boss, going on to become the first woman on Lamboo to break the cycle and put an end to generations of female inequality.

Outside her life on Lamboo Station, sport was important to Darrylin and she had a passion—and a talent—for basketball. Throughout high school, which she attended in the local town, she competed in tournaments and carnivals across the Kimberley region before eventually travelling to other towns for competitions. She says she used basketball as her emotional outlet and thrived on the adrenaline and the competition. As the years went on, it was soon clear that Darrylin's talent for the sport was more than just a hobby. When she was seventeen years old, she caught the eye of a well-known recruiter in Western Australia and was offered the opportunity of a lifetime—a scholarship to play professional basketball for a team based in Perth. However, the day she was due to meet with her recruiter and accept the contract offer, she discovered something that suddenly put the handbrake on her entire life and future plans. She was pregnant. In an instant, Darrylin's future as a professional athlete was off the table. She decided without hesitation to continue with the pregnancy and focus on her new role as a mother.

'I had no regrets. Yes, it was disappointing about my basketball career but spiritually I felt a connection to this baby even before the first ultrasound.'

Darrylin and her then-partner, the father of her child, were happily dating at the time and were committed to raising their baby together. In 2008, Darrylin gave birth to a beautiful little boy they named Hafiz, and the three of them settled into family life on Lamboo Station, with plenty of support from Darrylin's family including her mum, who was a nurse. When I think back to when I was eighteen years old, there's no way I was emotionally ready to become a mother, and Darrylin admits it was a tough transition to begin with. At the time, her friends were busy doing what eighteen-year-olds do, enjoying their freedom, partying and planning their future careers. Meanwhile, Darrylin had taken on the biggest responsibility of her life at home and was forced to grow up very quickly. While she loved being a mum, she says she did struggle mentally at times and craved getting out of the house and away from her domestic responsibilities. She could see her brothers working on the station and felt a pang of jealousy, hoping that one day she could get out there and be part of that world too.

A pivotal moment for Darrylin came following some stern comments from Jabi, who was always one of her biggest supporters. Professionally, he saw enormous potential in her at an early age and could see she was feeling frustrated as a new mum, wanting to get out in the world and do more than simply fulfilling her role at home. She was struggling more than she cared to admit to herself at the time and credits her granddad for pulling her out of her mental slump. His brief but impactful pep talk came one day when he stopped by to chat to Darrylin while she was sitting on the couch feeding six-month-old Hafiz. She'd been whingeing about how she was feeling when he suddenly snapped her out of the deep-seated beliefs about being a mum that had paralysed her.

'He said, "What are you doing?" And I said, "I'm feeding the baby, I'm a stay-at-home mum." He said, "No, the world doesn't stop just because you're a mum. Get out there, get a job, provide. I know you want to!"'

Darrylin spent the next couple of years working part time at a local women's shelter in the nearby town of Halls Creek, supporting victims of domestic violence. She loved the work. It gave her purpose and she was passionate about giving back to the community. Then, when Hafiz was four years old, Darrylin left Lamboo Station and moved to Darwin with her partner in a quest to push herself and find herself. However, eight months into their new life in the Northern Territory, Darrylin received the devastating news that her granddad, her beloved Jabi, had been diagnosed with cancer. Darrylin immediately made arrangements to return to Lamboo to be with him and she hasn't left the station since.

On 11 June 2015, Darrylin's grandfather passed away surrounded by his family at home on Lamboo and was laid to rest at a family burial site on the property. Darrylin remembers their last few days together fondly. Until his final breath, all their conversations centred around Lamboo and future plans and ideas that would improve the family's cattle enterprise. In the years after he died, Darrylin continued to work off the station in various roles, including as a community engagement officer at the local council and then as a cultural adviser with the Western Australian police force. Over the years, she would also take time off to work to spend a few months working on Lamboo during the mustering season, much to the disgust of many of the male workers, but she'd had her father's and her grandfather's blessing, so they didn't have a say. Each time the mustering season ended, Darrylin found it harder and harder to go back to town to work. Lamboo was in her blood; with her granddad's voice constantly echoing inside her, she just couldn't shake the feeling that she belonged there permanently.

'Since I was a young girl, Jabi would always say to me, "Just you wait. One day you're going to run this station! I believe in you!"'

Darrylin grew more and more curious and started thinking that she could carve out a career for herself on Lamboo. What was stopping her? Her gender shouldn't matter. When her grandmother passed away two years after Jabi and was laid to rest next to him, Darrylin decided it was time for her to make her move, to begin her campaign to take on the management of the station and help secure the future that her grandfather had envisioned for her and for the land.

'My grandfather was my biggest supporter. I wanted to make him proud. Having them buried here is a constant reminder to me that we need to nurture the station and push for a brighter future.'

> Since I was a young girl, Jabi would always say to me, 'Just you wait. One day you're going to run this station! I believe in you!'

Over the years, Darrylin gradually developed her business skills, taking part in the annual Indigenous Cattle Producer's Workshop organised by the Department of Agriculture and Food. There, she learned the fundamentals of farming business—financial planning and management, animal nutrition and sustainable land management. Her uncle had been the manager of Lamboo for many years before he abruptly left the station in 2019. When his time came to an end, Darrylin immediately seized the opportunity and put her hand up for the top job. After years of doubting whether it would ever be possible, her dream to run the station was suddenly within reach, even if no one else saw it that way at the time.

'I stood up to a lot of people who undermined women's strengths and it was tough, especially for me as an Indigenous woman and all the judgemental shit you have to cop.'

Darrylin was told countless times that she was too young for the role, too inexperienced and that she didn't have what it took to lead the business. But deep down, that bias came down to one simple thing: her gender and the deeply ingrained beliefs within her family and her culture. She had to fight hard to have her voice heard. She says that for a First Nations woman to challenge any man at anything can be deemed culturally disrespectful and inappropriate. Even some people within her own community deeply disapproved of her mission to become manager, but Darrylin didn't let it stop her.

'I had people say to me, "Well you can't be the manager because you're a girl." I copped backlash. But I don't tolerate that sort of bullshit anymore. I've earned that respect.'

In 2019, a 28-year-old Darrylin formally advised the Board of Directors at Ngunjiwirri Aboriginal Corporation, which owns Lamboo, that she would be applying for the role of station manager. The board oversees the running of the business and would ultimately decide Darrylin's fate. But informally it was the blokes out on the station who needed the most convincing. Darrylin's desire for the top job led to an enormous amount of jealousy within her family. So she did what any fearless and unstoppable woman would do; she challenged them to a 'farm-off' (I just made that term up but you get the drift). She put it to them that if any of them thought they deserved the role of manager more than she did, then they could go ahead and prove it by going head-to-head with her in a competition that would test who had the better skills. From mustering, fencing, concreting and even car mechanics, Darrylin was ready to take them all on, but she didn't have to. Darrylin's family knew that she was the best man and woman for the job, even though it broke with tradition, and the board of directors agreed. A few months later, Darrylin stepped up to become the first female manager in the business's 24-year history, and the first woman to challenge the status quo and break the cycle that up until that point had a strong hold on Lamboo.

'It was an incredible feeling. Now, I love it when I see a man with ego. I'm like, yeah, you and I are going to work together today because I want to break that shit down.'

Darrylin manages up to ten staff on Lamboo during the cattle season, with the business growing its herd from just 300 head of Brahman-cross to 2500 in 2022. There is no typical day on the station for Darrylin. She's a master of all trades, overseeing operations and getting her hands dirty with everything from mustering right through to the more mundane managerial tasks of paperwork and keeping on top of the business's finances. Darrylin admits it's taken her some time to find her feet and claim her confidence as the boss, and there have been some awkward moments where the lines between her family life and work life have been difficult to separate.

'When I first started, it was so weird telling my dad to do what I wanted to do, because he's the longest-serving worker on the station—he's been here his whole life. So, when he questioned me, I was like, wait a minute, you're questioning me? I'm not asking you; I'm telling you to do that.'

For all the struggles and backlash she has faced over the years, perhaps the biggest change when it comes to Darrylin's story is not the title she now holds out on the station but the shift in mindset from her family and staff. Darrylin is building a new workplace culture and a new generation of First Nations farmers and workers in her region and on her land. They are learning to respect women more and understand that it is possible for women in agriculture to play a significant role in the operational side of farming businesses, while also respecting their culture. There's one particular male in her life who has always supported her and who has probably not been game enough to question her out on the station: her thirteen-year-old son, Hafiz. He's grown up watching his mum challenge the status quo and smash stereotypes and he's often out on horseback or in the yards with his mum, watching, learning and helping. While Darrylin admits her son has often been dragged along for the ride by her and is at an age where he'd sometimes prefer to be at home playing video games rather than be out on the station in the piercing heat, Hafiz has thrived in the outback with his family, learning all the skills his mum learned at the same age.

There's a reason they say it takes a village to raise a child and there's no doubt Darrylin has relied heavily on hers over the years. Understanding what Darrylin has been able to achieve and overcome out on the station as a young mum—not just professionally but logistically—is important when it comes to acknowledging how rural mums need to be supported in their chosen pathways should they wish to seek employment, particularly in agriculture. There aren't many jobs where you can take your child to work, let alone have a family babysitting service on standby to help you when you need, but these are the things Darrylin has relied on to chase her dreams. She's leaned on her family throughout her motherhood journey, spending many weeks away for meetings in the city and many hours cooped up working in the office on the station, relying on her family (siblings, aunties and cousins) to look after her son. In many ways, Darrylin has been able to experience motherhood in the same way that her ancestors did, bringing Hafiz up within a community and within a family that lives together on the same property.

In First Nations culture, raising a child was the responsibility of the entire village. Today, we parent in an individualistic culture where the responsibility falls on two primary carers, Mum and Dad. Darrylin told me that without her family she wouldn't be where she is today, and while she can't imagine raising ten children like her grandmother did, she understands and appreciates how different times were back then.

'Every woman chipped in on raising the children. The respect and the connectedness—I love that because it kept everybody together. But then generations just started changing.'

Darrylin is surrounded by her parents, her sister and her cousins on the station, and everyone has their own home and their own space. But the reassurance of having that support close by whenever she needs has enabled Darrylin to break free from the confines of tradition.

'Sometimes I hate having such a big family where everyone knows everyone's business. But when I think of Hafiz and motherhood, I've been able to become the mum I am today because I've had that support.'

Darrylin recently separated from Hafiz's father and it's been difficult to settle into co-parenting life, with Hafiz now sharing his time between the station and the town of Halls Creek where his father lives. However, that arrangement won't last very long as Darrylin is now preparing for a completely new chapter as a mum. Hafiz is heading off to boarding school in Darwin where he'll be based for the next six years through high school, and who knows what he'll do after that. Darrylin secretly (but also now very publicly) hopes Lamboo will one day lure him home.

Sometimes I hate having such a big family where everyone knows everyone's business. But when I think of Hafiz and motherhood, I've been able to become the mum I am today because I've had that support.

Regardless, Darrylin is focusing on her future and the future of the land she has been entrusted with. With a promising future career on the horizon as a trailblazing leader, she has no plans to leave the land. Her grandfather, her Jabi, is forever the voice in her head pushing her to get out of her comfort zone and continue to improve the operation. She has fought so hard to get to this position and feels that she has an obligation to the land, to her ancestors and to future generations. Darrylin is also passionate about growing the Lamboo Station enterprise and inspiring the next generation of First Nations farmers, particularly females, by supporting them into the agricultural industry. She plans to develop a three-month training program to help local residents across the region develop the skills they need to get local jobs in the farming sector or in other industries such as mining and tourism right across Western Australia.

There's no stopping this woman. Seriously, listen to our conversation back on episode 112 of the *Motherland* podcast, and you can hear it plain as day in her voice. She is a woman on a mission. And while she was once a little girl who constantly heard 'You can't' and 'You shouldn't' from those around her, she's now in the driver's seat, championing other young women and inspiring the next generation of First Nations changemakers with the words 'You can' and 'You will'. And she has.

'When I think back to that little girl running around the bush barefoot, with really dry brown–blondish desert-looking hair . . . I just never thought I'd be who I am today.'

# 4

# Pat Fennell: What you can do with twenty quid

## Mount Isa, Queensland

I can usually persuade almost anyone to have a yarn with me and I spent most of my TV career doing just that. But one of the biggest struggles I've had with the *Motherland* podcast is persuading rural women in their seventies or eighties to open up about their lives and their motherhood journey. They've raised kids on the land in a totally different era and have a wealth of experience to share, but, whether it's a generational thing or I've simply been unlucky, many of these women are hesitant to open up publicly. They like to keep things private, especially when it comes to the struggles they've encountered.

Pat Fennell isn't one of those women. At 89 years of age, she is an open book. She's been a disgraced divorcee in an era of inequality for women, a single mum, a working mum and a fierce advocate for the cattle industry and for remote health. Oh, and she retired and then unretired at the age of 66. She has seen and done so much in her extraordinary life and she has no hesitation in talking openly about it all. Nothing is off limits.

'I want my children to know the truth about their mum and dad, warts and all. I hope that some of those experiences will help them when they are confronted with issues in their lives.'

Pat was born in 1933 in the rural town of Charleville in Queensland, some 700 kilometres west of Brisbane. She spent two years of her early life living with her parents and her little brother in the bush, camping in roadside tents. Her father was a time clerk for the Main Roads Department, which was busy building multiple new highways across western Queensland. Their family's nomadic lifestyle was part of the package; they went where there was work and, depending on where they were stationed, the mail truck usually arrived once a week, bringing them food supplies. They'd take enough food for a couple of days and store the meat in a hanging safe in the breeze to ensure it stayed cool, burying the rest of their fresh food in a hole for preservation, a metre underground. These were vastly different times and, although Pat's family struggled financially, she says she had a wonderful childhood with incredible parents who made the whole experience one big adventure. When World War II began, Pat's father was conscripted into the Civil Constructional Corps (CCC), a civilian-based labour force designed to organise military construction works. He was tasked with assisting in developing roads and railways for the defence sector in Shorncliffe, a coastal suburb in Brisbane. Pat and her family lived there until she was eight years old, and though she and her brother were shielded as much as possible from the devastation of the war, a constant awareness of it surrounded them.

'I had such wonderful parents. They told us as much as we needed to know without alarming us. We understood there was a war going on because we heard it on the radio each night and they listened to it with intensity.'

Pat's mother taught her kindergarten remotely before the family moved back to Charleville permanently in 1941 and Pat started at the local primary school. She adored learning—a passion that stayed with her for her entire life. She was so bright that she ended up skipping Grade 2 and jumping straight to Grade 3. Back then, Pat's dream was to become a doctor, but she quickly realised the dream was unattainable as fate had other plans for her family. Their finances became very strained after Pat's father Bill had the first of several strokes that eventually prevented him from working full time. By the time Pat started high school, their situation was dire, and at just fourteen years old she had to drop out of school to work and contribute financially to help her family make ends meet.

Pat got a job at the local council and eventually moved up to be a senior clerk working 45 hours a week. She continued to work there until she was eighteen, doing everything from cashier work, taking minutes at council meetings and sending out rates notices or balancing ledgers. On the weekends, Pat also took on a part-time radio announcing job in the evenings, managing a dinner program that played classical music from 6–7 pm. Pat was forced to grow up very quickly and there was no stopping her once she got a taste for working life and the means to provide for her family.

'It was very hard and times were tight. There was no money. The family was dependent on my wages, so I did what I had to do.'

It was during Pat's career in radio that she met a man named Rex who changed her life forever. He was fifteen years her senior and it didn't take long for Pat to fall in love with the mature, smooth-talking, handsome radio announcer. They kept their whirlwind secret romance under wraps for several months until Pat could no longer contain her happiness, openly declaring her love for him. But at nineteen years old, Pat found out she was pregnant, something she and Rex hadn't planned, and she was immediately made to feel deeply ashamed. In those days, in the fifties, women didn't have access to the contraceptive pill and many young women, like Pat, weren't given any parental guidance on sex or contraception. Straight away, Rex offered his hand in marriage (as was customary in those days in that situation), and they married soon after at the local registry office.

> The family was dependent on my wages, so I did what I had to do.

Rex had served in the merchant navy during World War II, and in many ways returned a broken man. While there were no issues in their relationship early on, as Pat's pregnancy progressed, the red flags soon became too obvious to ignore.

'We just couldn't make it work. He had a kind heart but a lot of mental issues that resulted from war and that's why I hate war so much.'

Rex worked as a painting contractor throughout their marriage but any savings or disposable income vanished quickly. He had an alcohol addiction and spent many hours drinking at the local pub. After a particularly nasty argument, Pat finally decided enough was enough. Rex returned home to find his belongings packed and waiting for him near the garage door. This was an exceptionally bold move for Pat given the times.

Both her Presbyterian upbringing and society's expectations meant marriage was supposed to be forever no matter what, but despite trying very hard to stick it out, Pat followed her instinct, knowing deep down she couldn't have a happy life with this man. Heavily pregnant, Pat filed for divorce and prepared to face motherhood alone—a decision that flew in the face of everything society expected of her.

'It was a terrible disgrace to be divorced. Nobody wanted to know you! Divorcee was spelled in capital letters in those days because it was very rare and frowned upon.'

Pat tried to ignore the external pressures and judgement, and with the loving and unwavering support of her parents, focused on the arrival of her baby. On Tuesday, 4 August 1953, Pat's beautiful little girl Kerryn was born, and Pat says that the moment she met her precious daughter all the pain, embarrassment and stress of the past couple of years simply evaporated.

'It was just beautiful when I held the little girl in my arms and the priest came up and he said, "Oh, well, it's all over." I said, "No Father, it's just the beginning."'

Pat's maternal instinct blossomed and she vowed that she would give her daughter everything she possibly could in life. Ten days after Kerryn's birth, Pat was back at work at the council office, and soon after that she enrolled in an accountancy course to study bookkeeping so she could upskill and ensure she had even more financial security to support her little girl. For the first few years of motherhood, Pat didn't do anything but work. It wasn't until Kerryn turned three that Pat finally had the confidence to go out socially, and her first outing was to the annual Charleville Show in 1956. It's there that she reconnected with Mark Fennell, a man she'd gone to primary school with, years prior. Mark confessed to Pat that he'd fallen in love with her at thirteen years old, when they were at the local skating rink with friends. Back then, he had decided that he would marry her one day. It took several years for them to rekindle their friendship, but eventually Pat fell in love with him too. Mark proposed and, for all the right reasons, Pat said yes.

Soon after marrying, Pat was introduced to rural life. Mark was from a grazing family and they moved to one of the family properties, Footscray Station, near Winton. An extremely remote station with no electricity and no telephone, it was 1200 kilometres north-west of Brisbane. The newlyweds didn't own much but their clothes, a secondhand ute and an old blitz truck when they arrived. They found a used spring bed (minus the legs), a stretcher and a couple of mattresses that they loaded up and took with them on the 700-kilometre journey from Charleville to their new home. Pat got to work trying to turn their new, bare house into a home. She placed their bed on top of four oil drums and cultivated the veggie garden to grow as much of their own food as possible.

Despite the challenges, the young couple were extremely happy with their new life and wanted for nothing. Within a few months of moving to the station, Pat was pregnant, and in June 1959 they welcomed their healthy little boy, Alan.

'Love conquers all, so who cares if you don't have money or possessions?'

Pat and her family lived on Footscray Station for twelve months before an opportunity to run their own property came up. Linda Downs Station was 2000 square kilometres of undeveloped, rugged country right on the Queensland and Northern Territory border, one of the most isolated parts of the country. Mark's father bought the property under a ballot system after World War I, and it was to be jointly owned by his two sons. However, Mark's brother, who had three small children at the time, said he wasn't interested in moving out there because it was too remote, but Mark and Pat decided they were willing to have a crack. 'We moved out there with a little girl, a six-week-old baby and twenty quid in the pocket.'

Pat likens their transport to Linda Downs as something that would rival Noah's ark. They packed everything they could fit, and set out with several pigs, a couple of goats, eight hens and a rooster—all animals that were to feed their growing family. Alan was a newborn when they made the three-day voyage through the gruelling Aussie outback. They stopped regularly so Pat could breastfeed and they dropped into a stock camp where they were greeted by graziers with drinks and warm food to fill their bellies.

At last, the old broken-down homestead of Linda Downs came into view. Their new home was underserviced, with no electricity, telephones or running water. Mark got to work installing water bores across the property for the cattle and making their living arrangements more comfortable. He ran a pipe into the kitchen, cutting a 44-gallon drum in half, chiselling a hole into the base and plumbing it up to use as their kitchen sink. As for what Pat could cook in their makeshift kitchen, well that is another story! With no mail service to their property, their diet was almost entirely free of fresh fruit and vegetables. They relied solely on fresh meat from animals that they killed and prepared themselves, plus potatoes, onions, peas and beans that they grew and stored. For their nutritional hit of calcium, Pat milked the goats every day.

Linda Downs Station enjoyed 250 millimetres of rain each year and was great fattening country for cattle. Unfortunately, it was also riddled with the poisonous *Acacia georginae*, a native tree that is deadly to cows if they eat it. In good seasons, when grass was plentiful, it usually wasn't a problem. However, during one dry spell the plant was too much of a temptation for hungry cattle and Mark and Pat lost more than half of their 300 cows. Looking back now, Pat says she can't believe how she and Mark could possibly have thought that they could make something of a poison-riddled property on their own with no money and no clue.

'We set off with brains the size of a pea and hearts the size of Phar Lap's!' Pat recalls with a chuckle.

There's no doubt that life on Linda Downs was tough at times for the bold young couple. While he already had his hands full at home, Mark would also venture out to the bush each year to earn some extra money as a contract musterer, rounding up cattle on horseback and camping in the outback for several weeks at a time. Pat remembers the first time she was left alone on the station with the kids. As she waved goodbye to Mark, she suddenly felt loneliness seeping into her. Her nearest neighbour being 30 kilometres away, Pat felt incredibly alone, but the chaos of taking care of her children helped pass the time very quickly until Mark returned home.

When I think back to my life with a toddler and a newborn, and all the luxuries I have enjoyed raising my two children—warm running water, power, phone signal and Netflix—it's incredible to think how different life on the land was for mothers like Pat. Pat's generation often has a very 'just get on with it' attitude and there's a certain resilience and hardiness about them that makes me feel guilty for whingeing about my life or motherhood at all! But there's also a softness under Pat's tough exterior that I adore. She talks openly about the hard times and the loneliness she felt as a rural mother—something so many of us can relate to, whether raising kids in 1953 or 2023.

We set off with brains the size of a pea and hearts the size of Phar Lap's!

Pat went on to have four children—Kerryn, Alan, Kim and Kalinda. Raising them all at Linda Downs was extremely isolating at times. The only other people who lived full time at the original Linda Downs site were Jimmy, an Aranda man, and Johnny Bookie. Later, after building and moving to what became known in the family as 'New Linda Downs', situated on the Georgina River, there were two Aranda families who lived on the property permanently. At mustering time, the workforce could swell to ten people to manage the mustering, maintenance of waters and so on.

Her thirst for learning made Pat a gifted teacher. She taught all four of her kids through distance education for their primary school years before they each headed off to boarding school in Charters Towers. Today, homeschooling is much more sophisticated for most rural families, having been revolutionised by access to phones, the internet, video-conferencing capabilities and regular communication with teachers. However, for Pat, homeschooling in the sixties was a very different experience. Everything was done on hardcopy, with weekly instructions and homework sent by snail mail to the station every few weeks or months.

'It was all pretty primitive. There were a couple of pages of instructions for English, maths and history but the rest was up to your imagination. At Christmas time, during the wet season, they'd send six weeks of work so you didn't run out, because some of the rivers ran and we couldn't get any mail out to the station.'

Pat's love of teaching soon expanded beyond the family classroom to include children of the Aboriginal workers and indeed some of their parents who had not had the benefit of any formal education. One female employee on the station, also a mum, received a doctor's report in the mail about her child who'd recently been sick. After talking to Pat, the woman admitted that she couldn't comprehend a word of the report because she'd never been taught to read or write. That's when Pat stepped in and offered to teach her.

'She said, "Do you think I can learn, missus? I'm 35." I said, "Of course you can!" We started with the alphabet and we went from there.'

It was these opportunities that Pat embraced, and she was rewarded with lifetime friendships.

As Mark and Pat's family grew bigger and busier, so did their grazing empire. Less than ten years after arriving in the region, Mark and Pat had built one of the most extensive station complexes in the north-west region, consisting of fully air-conditioned, modern homesteads for their family and their workers, along with machinery sheds and other farming structures. They also doubled their land holdings by purchasing Roxborough, a 2000-square-kilometre property that adjoined Linda Downs. Through continuing to fatten and trade cattle, Mark and Pat went on to purchase two more properties in north-west Queensland.

While Mark focused on building their business, Pat was finding her purpose outside motherhood and station life. Over time, she found her passion in rural advocacy. While at Old Linda Downs she had joined the Country Women's Association Urandangi branch, and she later became secretary and eventually president. The ladies of the CWA worked tirelessly to raise funds for causes around the region, including the Ruth Fairfax Home, which provided accommodation for rural women who needed to visit Brisbane to access various services. The other critical role Pat's CWA branch provided, along with all the branches across Australia, was a social outlet for women who had few chances to network with other women when their neighbours could be hours away by car and many didn't have a telephone.

Once all four of her children were at boarding school, Pat decided to dedicate all her spare time to increasing her efforts to become a voice for rural Australia, fighting for more equality across the community. She started by tackling one of the most male-dominated industry bodies in the country—the Cattleman's Union of Australia. In the eighties, Pat worked her way up to become the first female president of its Mount Isa branch. She was also the first woman to be elected as a representative of Cattle Council Australia, which saw her rise to prominence in the industry, playing a key role in advocating for cattle producers across the country. Pat argued for the benefits of the live cattle exports to Indonesia, which was worth hundreds of millions of dollars to the Australian economy each year, and in 1995 she helped organise a live cattle forum in Karumba, Queensland, securing sponsorships and attracting 400 people to discuss the live cattle trade. A ministerial advisory committee was set up immediately after the forum and Pat was promptly appointed advisor to Bob Gibbs, who was Minister for Primary Industries at the time.

'It was one of the best things I was involved in. I even got to travel to the Philippines as part of a trade mission which was a big eye-opener!'

If you think Pat's CV is already looking impressive, that's not the half of it. In 2020, she received a Medal of the Order of Australia (OAM) in the Queen's Birthday Honours List for her years of lobbying for equality for people in the bush. She's been a fierce advocate for rural and remote health, serving on the Women's Council for Rural and Regional Communities where she lobbied to have Indigenous Liaison Officers appointed at

Mount Isa Hospital for the first time. She was also integral in the development of the Centre for Rural and Remote Health, a training centre for young health professionals in Mount Isa. Her deep understanding and respect for Aboriginal culture, stemming from her time at Linda Downs, pushed her to fight for equality in education and a complete overhaul of nursing traineeships in the region. Traditionally, all nurse trainees had to travel away from the Mount Isa region to undertake hospital traineeships but, after lobbying and collaborating with a local doctor, Pat secured the first group of nurse trainees at Mount Isa Hospital, and six of the eight were First Nations people.

'Aboriginal people generally don't like to leave their families, and you can't just change 60,000 years of culture because it suits our system. I wanted to improve local skills and provide more job opportunities for all people across our town and wider region.'

Pat has seen and done so much in her 89 years, and she admits that retiring has not been easy. Pat and Mark first tried their hand at retiring when they were aged 64. They went overseas to Europe and travelled the world for a few months, trying to get used to a slower pace of life. But, as it turns out, life in the slow lane wasn't for them. In 1997, their family was hit by a tragedy that rocked them so hard that Pat and Mark really lost their way. Their beloved granddaughter Katie was killed in a horrific water accident just a few kilometres north of

Linda Downs. Pat still remembers the chilling phone call she received that day.

'When her father rang me and said, "Katie's dead", my breath just left me and I stammered. I was completely incoherent and don't even remember what I said. We were utterly heartbroken.'

The months and years that followed were the hardest of their lives as Pat and Mark tried to cope with their grief and support the rest of the family. They continued to do some travelling, feeling lost and uncertain about their own future plans. Two years later, an opportunity popped up which saw them 'unretire' and chase a new career path together. They bought a local real estate agency and spent more than ten years working in the property market across north-west Queensland. Then, in their late seventies, they finally decided it was time to call it a day.

In recent years, Mark's health has taken a turn for the worse. He's been diagnosed with dementia and has been deteriorating rapidly. In 2021, Pat made the decision to move Mark into a local nursing home so he could get the care he needed. But their bond is such that Pat decided to move into the same facility and she lives just down the corridor from Mark, in the low-care part of the home. She visits her beloved Mark every afternoon, and although his memory is fading she still sits with him for hours, talking, reading to him, bringing him his favourite treats and showing him pictures of their grandkids on her phone. Some days he's responsive but others he doesn't recognise his dear old Patsy. They've been married for 64 years and they've been inseparable. The secret to their everlasting love?

'We each have something that the other needed in their life. Mark gave me the opportunity to break free from a life that was going to be very hard and he chose to love me and gave me a chance at a better world. In return, I have offered him my unconditional love and loyalty and I've guided him through our businesses and our life together. He's dyslexic so he's needed me a lot at times, especially to get all the paperwork done for our real estate licence, let me tell you!'

Pat and I have kept in touch regularly since I first interviewed her for the podcast. She's sent me some of her poetry, inspired by her life on the land with Mark and by her deep respect for the bush. The poem I love the most is the one she wrote about Mark, which she's allowed me to share with you at the end of this chapter. I teared up when she read it out loud. Their love and their bond is beautiful.

'You hear about the woman behind the man, but sometimes it's the other way around. We shouldn't forget that a combination of a man and a woman can beat the world.'

Every time I hang up the phone after one of my chats with Pat, I feel invigorated and fuelled with gratitude. Yes, life can be tough; Pat knows that as well as anyone, but she has a beautiful way of stating the bleeding obvious. And whenever she feels a pang of sadness or when the walls of the nursing home begin to close in on her, she ventures out to the land. Two of her daughters live on properties in the region and she'll often wander over and sit by the river where she breathes in the fresh air and gives thanks for her wonderful life.

'Happiness is wanting what you get, not getting what you want. Because what you get is going to be what you have, so you may as well be happy with that and do something with it.'

> We shouldn't forget that a combination of a man and a woman can beat the world.

## LOVE LETTERS

### Pat Fennell

I'm typing your love letters, and my dear it makes me sad,
But it also does remind me that I really should feel glad.
Glad to have these precious thoughts of your sweet love for me
The greatest gift from a loving man that ever a wife did see.
They tell the story of the time we had to spend apart
For you to earn a living and get a fitting start
To a life for us together, what wondrous plans you had,
And you shared it with your darling girl—it made my heart so glad.
And whilst waiting for our wedding day, my pride in you just grew
Knowing in my heart that you always would come through
On all those precious promises you made so faithfully.
And looking back, I truly know, they really came to be.
Promise of a better life, lived fully side by side,
Promises of children dear, to fill our hearts with pride,
Promises to lend a hand, to any that we knew
Who needed some encouragement, their life dream to pursue.
I look back on the people whose many lives we've touched,
And if we feel we've sometimes failed, it doesn't matter much.
For through our lives, we've never tried to hurt a human being
Or to be cruel to an animal, or to be racist, or be mean.
We've tried to love our fellow man, that's sometimes a bit hard,
But we did our best, our very best, to achieve that last hard yard.

MACK

# 5

# Danyelle Haigh: Mother trucker

## Anmatjere, Northern Territory

It can often take me some time to pin down a rural mum for a chat. We're all juggling family life and farm life, and then throw some dodgy internet service into the mix. Most of the mums I interview at least have a permanent address—but not Danyelle Haigh. There is nothing conventional about Danyelle's life in the bush or her motherhood journey to date. When we finally catch up, she's pulled over on the side of the road, hooked up to satellite internet in her glimmering pink Mack truck while on the job near Camooweal in country Queensland.

For almost ten years, Danyelle has spent ten months of the year travelling around the most remote locations in Australia in a truck, navigating some of the toughest roads and terrain. She's raised her two boys on the road while living out of a shipping container on the back of the road trains that she and her husband haul around the outback. It's not the glamorous life this former beach babe from the Gold Coast had planned for herself, and it's taken some time to get used to.

'Even my family and friends, when they see what I do and how we live, and how my life has changed, they're gob-smacked.'

Danyelle grew up in the middle of a bustling Surfers Paradise on Queensland's Gold Coast. She spent her twenties studying to be a nurse and enjoying the beach, the nightlife and the shopping. But her anticipated path through life went out the window when she fell in love with a country boy. At the time, Danyelle was working full time, managing her mum's all-female traffic control business, managing roadworks across the Gold Coast region. The girls were known as the 'lollipop ladies', and when Danyelle headed off to work that summer morning she had no idea just how sweet her day would get.

Danyelle's job was to help her staff block off roads and manage traffic to make way for a huge asphalt truck that would be laying down fresh bitumen along a busy road. As the truck approached that morning, Danyelle locked eyes with Anthony Haigh, the man behind the wheel. Anthony managed the asphalt company and later that day, once he and his workers had finished the road upgrade, they all sat down for a break with Danyelle's team. Asphalt takes several hours to dry and it was during those hours before the roads could be opened up again that Danyelle and Anthony got chatting—more so a bubbly Danyelle, who says she was drawn to Anthony immediately and was eager to get to know him better. Eight years her senior, Anthony was initially a little hesitant but his reservations didn't last long. They got along like a house on fire.

'I was persistent, and eventually he gave in and agreed to go on our first date. It's crazy, just two months later we moved in together.'

After a whirlwind romance, Anthony and Danyelle left the Gold Coast, bought a small block of land and settled two-and-a-half hours away in Warwick in Queensland's south-east. Danyelle finished her nursing degree and secured a job at a local aged-care centre shortly afterwards, while Anthony was busy running his own excavation business. Professionally they were both happy, but privately they were going through a heartbreaking journey. After getting married, they were excited to start trying for a family, but this sent them down a long road of pain, disappointment and miscarriages. Five years into their battle to conceive, they were ready to give up hope and Danyelle's mental health was suffering.

'I got quite depressed, because you think to yourself, "What's wrong with me? Why? Why is this happening?" I felt like my body was letting me down.'

Danyelle and Anthony decided to try IVF, which involved them travelling almost three hours back to the Gold Coast for all their appointments. Doctors told them that they had just a 15 per cent chance of conceiving, which was devastating to hear. They persevered and the following year Danyelle fell pregnant with their miracle baby Heath, conceived from their first embryo transfer. However, after everything Danyelle and Anthony had been through to get to the point of having a viable, healthy pregnancy and baby, there were still challenges ahead. Danyelle was diagnosed with gestational diabetes late in her pregnancy, and just a few weeks before she was due to give birth to Heath her blood pressure levels climbed dangerously high; when her diabetes levels became uncontrollable and she became hyperglycaemic. At 34 weeks, she was rushed to hospital, and two weeks later, after both the baby and Danyelle had been stabilised, an emergency C-section was performed.

Danyelle's wry comment was: 'Either he was going to kill me or kill us both.'

Little Heath spent five days in the newborn intensive care unit, with doctors trying to get his jaundice and blood sugar levels under control. It was an emotional roller-coaster for Danyelle and the relief she felt when she was finally able to bring her little boy home was beyond words. Thankfully, Heath was a very laid-back baby, which would prove to be a godsend for Danyelle and Anthony, because a laid-back baby was exactly the type of child they needed to survive the next chapter they were about to embark on as a family. One year after becoming parents, Danyelle and Anthony said yes to an enormous work opportunity and a lifestyle decision that would change everything.

> Either he was going to kill me or kill us both.

During their time in Warwick, Anthony had met a local man who owned a water-drilling business helping drought-stricken farmers across outback Australia. Coming from a high rainfall area of Tasmania that's relatively drought-resilient, I'm a little embarrassed to admit that I had no idea what water-drilling entailed until I googled Danyelle's business and watched videos of their team in action. Basically, a huge drill, held up by a steel rig, is pounded as deep as 400 metres into the ground in an attempt to access the water that lies beneath. When water is found, a system of pipes and a pump is installed so farmers can use the bore water to fill their dams, water troughs and irrigation systems. Water is basically liquid gold, particularly during tough times and dry spells. The owner of the water-drilling business was in his seventies and preparing to retire. He'd employed Anthony on a fly-in, fly-out basis as a casual driller's offsider. In between his own working commitments, Anthony would travel across Queensland and interstate to transport water-drilling equipment and manage contract water-drilling jobs. In 2015, the owner finally decided it was time to call it a day. He wanted to hand the baton over to new owners who understood what was involved in the business and could take it on almost immediately. Anthony and Danyelle were the obvious choice. He tapped them on the shoulder and gave them the opportunity of a lifetime—the chance to own a thriving outback business. But to take the opportunity would mean they'd have to swap their hobby-farm life in Warwick for a unique lifestyle in the outback.

'Anthony came home one day and said, "This could be one hell of an adventure. Do you want to do it?" And after going over the finances and realising it was a nice profitable business, I said, "Why not!"'

But while Anthony knew what was in store for them, having spent time working in the business, learning the ropes, Danyelle had absolutely no idea what she'd signed up for when they packed their suitcases (along with baby Heath and a nappy bag) and hit the road.

'I was so naive. I had no idea it was going to be so hard, especially in those first two years while we got up and going.'

Anyone who manages their own business knows how tough it can be, but the challenges that Danyelle and Anthony have faced are quite remarkable. Running the water-drilling business means they service farmers across the north of Australia, and to do so, they are required to live on the road nearly full-time, setting up camp for a few days at one station before travelling hours, sometimes days, to the next contract location. Their home address? A couple of shipping containers on the back of their road train. They often have no phone signal and no internet and have made a makeshift home to house only the most crucial creature comforts and facilities.

The two enormous trucks carry seven shipping containers, with two-and-a-half of those containers converted into a bedroom, a bathroom, a laundry, an office and, in recent years, a schoolroom. The rest of the load is made up of several tonnes of water-drilling equipment including the drill rig, drill rods, two tool sheds, a massive compressor and a cage full of spare tyres.

Danyelle and Anthony have done their best to make their nomadic life as comfortable as possible, with big generators and water tanks on board that keep the power and shower pumping. But life became considerably more crammed on board the Haighs' road-train home as Heath has grown older and since Danyelle and Anthony's second miracle baby, little Theo, was born via IVF in 2019, five years after Heath. Theo was just three weeks old when Danyelle and Anthony wrapped up their 'parental leave' and headed back to the Northern Territory for their next drilling job. The family of four shared a bedroom inside one of the shipping containers, with Danyelle and Anthony in a double bed, Heath in a bunk bed and Theo, who had only recently grown out of his cot, also squeezing into the same room.

The challenge of coping with the intense sleep deprivation associated with having a newborn was made even trickier given their sleeping arrangements.

'It has been incredibly difficult. With all four of us packed into one room, when the baby woke up in the night crying, all of us were up! It was a bit stressful and exhausting, but we had no choice. This is our crazy life!'

Danyelle and Anthony love their life on the road and things have become slightly easier over the past couple of years with Heath now eight years old and Theo three. Both boys love nothing more than riding in the front of the Mack and Western Star trucks with their mum and dad—and they spend a lot of time doing it. With increasingly dry conditions and drought up north, more farmers than ever are desperate for water and that's meant Danyelle and Anthony's business has been booming. Many of the Haighs' clients have become their closest friends, welcoming them into their homes for a meal or offering them a more comfortable bed. When they are hired to hunt down water, they set up camp at the property and stay there until the job is done. They work across Queensland, the Northern Territory and Western Australia, boasting a 90 per cent success rate and setting up close to 100 bores every year, often in scorching conditions. This is no job for the faint-hearted, and the kids are right there by their side for every minute of it. Station by station, their road-train convoy of drilling equipment is helping drought-stricken producers across Australia. Danyelle says that nothing beats seeing the smile on the farmers' faces when they hit water, not to mention the excited screams from her kids when it comes gushing out of the pipe.

'You do what you have to do to provide a better life for your family. It's not an easy job—standing out in the sun in up to 50-degree heat, day in, day out—but it's totally worth it.'

Danyelle's unique rural experience of motherhood in the outback has been as frightening as it has been thrilling and rewarding. She's got the hang of it now but when I ask her if she remembers her first night on the road when Heath was just over twelve months old, she groans and says it was the worst night she's ever had as a mother. While they were driving to their first contract job in the middle of nowhere in Queensland, two-and-a-half hours from the nearest doctor, Heath became very sick with a high fever, asthma and a worm infection. It was the middle of the night and as a first-time mum Danyelle didn't know what to do. The reality of their isolation hit her hard in those moments.

'It was horrible; we were not prepared. All I had with me was Panadol and that was it. I cried multiple times. Having no phone service out there and not being able to call friends or family to vent, that first night was a huge reality check for me.'

As she drove through the night to find medical help, Danyelle wasn't sure she'd be able to cope with the isolation, especially for her kids. But when they agreed to buy the business, she had promised Anthony that she'd 'give it a go' for five years, and if she still didn't like life on the road after that, they'd move on to do something else. Personally, I think she was extremely generous, promising to stick it out for five years! But that's Danyelle—tough and willing to give anything a go. As it turns out, while it took a couple of years, their new trucking life grew on her and she eventually fell in love with the freedom of the wide-open road and the adventures they could have as a family. Now, she even has a thing for big trucks, recently buying her own Mack track to drive, but we'll get to that in a bit!

> It was horrible, we were not prepared. All I had with me was Panadol and that was it . . . Having no phone service out there and not being able to call friends or family . . . that first night was a huge reality check for me.

To be frank, living this kind of isolated life with two young kids, sharing a bedroom and having limited communications or entertainment sounds bloody awful to me. Then I remember that

I'm the former city girl who couldn't go a day without wearing make-up and who thought she couldn't survive without Uber Eats, but here I am, loving my new country life and never wanting to go back to everything I once knew. Rural life is sneaky like that—it can creep up on you and steal your city-slicker heart if you allow it to. Danyelle could simply have chosen to base herself with the kids on their Warwick property while Anthony ran the water-drilling business and lived away from them for most of the year, as many FIFO workers do. Then Danyelle would have had a fixed address, a reliable phone service, internet and a bedroom all to herself. Heaven, right? *Wrong*. This family is one hell of a team and from the get-go Danyelle has refused to allow their business ventures to separate them.

'If we did that, we wouldn't see Anthony for months on end and that wasn't the life we were willing to give our children or ourselves. These kids have an amazing life and we love being a family unit. I'm happiest when we're all together so it was non-negotiable.'

Persisting with a nomadic life with two growing boys has presented many logistical parenting challenges for Danyelle, particularly with schooling. So, what do you do when your business and your only source of income relies on your family living on the back of a truck and travelling full time? Well, you create a school for them, and you eventually find someone to help you! When Heath was five years old, he was enrolled in kindergarten through Alice Springs School of the Air. There are several of these correspondence schools across Australia and they cater specifically for kids in remote and outback areas, conducting classes online or by phone (back in the day, they were held over UHF radio!). Danyelle and Anthony have converted one of the shipping containers into a purpose-built schoolroom. Danyelle initially tried her hand at managing the business, the curriculum *and* teaching Heath herself but she soon found out that it was best for everyone if she stepped down from the teacher role.

'I said to Anthony, I can't do this. I'm going to go mad and he's going to fail because I wasn't born to be a teacher.'

They decided it was time to seek extra support from a full-time governess to help Heath through his remote learning years. It's quite common for homeschooled rural children to have this type of support person or teacher—if their family is lucky enough to find one, that is! And the Haigh family's particular position description was very different to the usual governess job posting, so attracting someone to the role wasn't going to be easy. Danyelle needed to find someone who was not only a good teacher but who could also cope with extreme isolation and the lack of services that came with their life on the road. Not only that, this person would need to get along with the kids and the rest of the working camp too, particularly outside the classroom because, well, there aren't many places you can hide when you and your boss share a shipping container for a lunchroom and also sit around an intimate campfire every night for dinner, with the bush as your backdrop. There's no doubt that this type of remote lifestyle is not for everyone and it has been difficult for Danyelle to find a governess willing to stick it out long term. Heath's first governess stayed one year, while the next one stayed for two. When Danyelle and I caught up to chat about this book, she told me a third governess was on her way, with Heath about to start Grade Three. This is not a job for the faint-hearted and I'd call it extreme teaching!

'I never paint a pretty picture for anyone. I say it's hard. You won't have phone service, you will be isolated: that's the gig. We are lucky. We've had some beautiful governesses take a leap of faith and support us these past few years.'

Although they live off the grid for weeks at a time, Danyelle is adamant that she's gained far more riches out on the land than the material ones she's sacrificed and left behind on the Gold Coast. And when you speak with her, when you get a taste of her world, the incredible adventures and opportunities a life like this presents are crystal clear. The solitude can make life feel simpler and more peaceful. There's no traffic, no noise, no stress. While testing at times, living in such proximity to each other enables more meaningful connections and conversations. And when it comes to the childhood her kids have been gifted, there is no doubt that they have hit the jackpot, spending every day with their mum and dad, with thousands of hectares as their playground, meeting new friends every day along the way. The freedom and autonomy have Danyelle hooked. Running the business alongside Anthony has enabled her to take risks and do things she never in her wildest dreams saw herself doing.

For the first couple of years, Anthony drove one of their road-train trucks while an employee drove the other. In addition to a driver, they also had to hire another person to assist Anthony with the water drilling because it was proving difficult to find someone who was both willing and capable of driving the truck as well as doing the drilling. It came to a point recently where the additional cost of labour just wasn't making financial sense and that's when, with Anthony's encouragement, Danyelle was pushed out of her comfort zone yet again. She'd been quite happy in the passenger seat of their road trains over the years and had only ever driven an automatic car. But Anthony asked her if she'd consider getting her road-train licence and driving one of their trucks full time. It would save them a lot of money if Danyelle stepped up to the role.

'Initially it terrified me, thinking about pulling a hundred tons of equipment, millions of dollars of gear behind me, and travelling over these horrible roads. But I took the leap and got behind the wheel and had a crack!'

Later Danyelle agreed to keep driving full time for their business on one very important condition.

'I said to Anthony, "If you buy me the truck I want and I can paint it pink, I'll do it."'

So, these days, when Danyelle's on the road, you'll see her behind the wheel of her hot- pink custom Mack truck. She's smashing gender stereotypes one kilometre at a time, showing her two boys that you don't need to be a man to drive a road train and she loves it. Danyelle's new passion for trucks has led to some interesting marketing opportunities for their business too. The Haighs attracted the attention of TV show *Outback Truckers,* which covers the ups and the downs of transporters as they endeavour to convey goods and services on time across the country in some of the most treacherous conditions. Danyelle and Anthony have recently finished filming their fifth season, with another secret reality–documentary TV show in the works.

'Everyone seems to love seeing a family providing water to animals and the farmers that need it. Viewers also love watching us try not to kill each other because we're so secluded and isolated!'

I said to Anthony, 'If you buy me the truck
I want and I can paint it pink, I'll do it.'

In the meantime, when the cameras aren't rolling, Danyelle has been busy setting up the next chapter of her life. After almost a decade living on the road, she and Anthony have finally realised the dream of owning their own station and have relocated from Queensland to the Northern Territory to enjoy a more permanent postal address between their water-drilling jobs and to be based closer to many of the regions they service. In 2021, they took on a 2000-hectare farm 150 kilometres north of Alice Springs near a tiny town called Ti Tree. Danyelle's next project is to transform the station into a unforgettable outback experience to give guests an authentic, real farm-stay experience.

'Everywhere we go now for work is within a day's drive, which I love, so while we'll still be drilling, we hope to be home more and that is going to be really special for us as a family.'

When we caught up to discuss this book, Danyelle also gave me a more personal update regarding her hopes for more children. She and Anthony are looking at starting another IVF round, with their hopes resting on the two frozen embryos they have left, some 3000 kilometres away from her home. She's all set for her upcoming appointments and I very much hope that by the time you read this she's preparing to introduce another beautiful baby to her incredible life as a mother trucker.

Over the years, Danyelle has overcome every challenge that's been thrown her way with incredible strength and enthusiasm. She is a brave woman who, let's be frank, has managed to stay sane and stay married while living in a shipping container in the middle of nowhere, raising two kids with no Netflix and no Wiggles to lean on for emergency parenting support. While writing her story, I've tried to put myself in her shoes, to imagine living a life like hers, but I'm not sure I'd be cut out for such an existence. Because while rural life has seeped into my blood, there are certain luxuries I'm not sure I could go without. After some of what I consider to be my toughest parenting days at home, I often think of mums like Danyelle. I smile with disbelief to myself as I put my children to bed (in their own rooms), pour myself a G&T and settle into my next trashy TV show on Netflix, feeling frustrated if it takes more than half a second to load. Danyelle, you are a saint.

# 6

# Catriona Rowntree: The FIFO farm wife

## South-west Victoria

When I sat down for the video call at my computer, clicked 'admit participant' and saw Catriona Rowntree smiling back at me, I felt a knot in my stomach. I was nervous.

You see, throughout my early career as a young TV news reporter, I had secretly idolised Catriona. While I spent my days in courtrooms, chasing criminals, rushing to the scene of car accidents and attending—let's face it—mostly depressing press conferences, I'd often daydream of travelling the world and working on a show like *Getaway*, being paid to explore the globe while sharing upbeat stories of people and places.

I'd grown up admiring Catriona's bubbly and beautiful persona on our TV screens; her presentation skills are inspiring, her enthusiasm is infectious and she seemed to play that presenter role so easily. However, years later, I have had the pleasure of discovering for myself that 'Australia's most travelled woman' has never played any role other than herself. She's truly one of the most authentic and down-to-earth women you'll ever meet. What you see on screen is what you get in real life. When she's not travelling the globe, she's a doting mum and a self-described 'accidental farmer's wife'. I had absolutely no idea about her personal story and how she ended up on the land, a world away from her home turf and TV studios in the city. It's one hell of an adventure!

'I accidentally fell in love with this really handsome farmer whose life is 110 per cent different to mine.'

Catriona lives on a sheep and grain property in south-west Victoria with her husband James and their two boys. But her rural retreat is not exactly the life she envisioned for herself as a self-confessed 'city chick'. While she adores her life, putting down roots in the country took several years of hard work, heartbreak and, eventually, a huge compromise. Catriona is a proud North Shore Sydney girl, the youngest of four children, who grew up 20 minutes from the heart of the city. She says she's been talkative and loud her whole life, desperate as a young girl to stand out in her busy, noisy household of six where being the centre of attention was nearly impossible.

Amongst the chaos of home life, Catriona found calm through the very special relationship and close bond she had with her beloved grandmother who was a guiding light throughout her life. Her nan was like a second mum to her, as well as a mentor and confidante who shaped many of the choices she made as a woman and as a mother. She was even the inspiration for one of Catriona's books, which shares the life lessons she'd learned at her nan's knee. When I asked Catriona about her motherhood journey raising her two boys, her stories are full of recollections of her nan's words of wisdom.

'She taught me to always choose kindness, and when you're a mother that is a verb . . . You've got to really focus on choosing kindness when your children are driving you up the wall!'

There's no doubt that kindness is a trait that has served Catriona well throughout her life and career; it's hard not to love her, and Australia agrees. She has spent 25 years at the helm of the country's most popular travel show, and it was a role she was born to play but fate needed a little push. Catriona's mum recognised in her outspoken, energetic, eight-year-old daughter the desire to stand out and promptly enrolled her in speech and drama classes. From there, her confidence and her talent grew into a force to be reckoned with.

While Catriona went on to become the golden girl of Australian television, she has worked incredibly hard and pushed through many challenges to get to where she is now.

Her ability to 'talk the leg off a chair' caused major issues for her in the classroom and nearly sent her life spiralling. At school, she was constantly in trouble for talking too much and disrupting the class, and she says that she spent a lot of time in detention. In Year 7, her first school suspended her indefinitely, a cataclysmic moment that could have defeated her, but instead it propelled her forward.

When Catriona changed schools, she was taken under the wing of the headmaster who, quite frankly, saw the bleedingly obvious talent she had, and instead of punishing her for it he helped her harness it and believe in it.

'He said, "OK, I can see that you just like to have a chat."

'My previous school said I was never going to amount to anything because I couldn't stop talking but this man looked at me and he said, "You never know, Catriona, one day you could get paid to do that."'

And that's exactly what happened. With the support of her new school, and a growing love of storytelling and journalism, Catriona's thirst for a career in broadcasting was unquenchable. After visiting a Sydney radio station where her friend's father was an announcer, Catriona pursued her passion relentlessly, and when she finished high school she secured her first job in community radio. Over the following three years she applied for countless jobs in the TV industry before finally, as she grew tired of sending out her resume with no success, she secured an audition with Channel Nine's children's series *Wonder World* and her climb to TV stardom began. In 1992 Catriona was a junior researcher on the show and by 1994 she was promoted to host. Two years after that, she got the biggest break of her career when she was hired as the face and host of the hit travel show *Getaway* and her career literally took off. She rummaged through her drawers for her passport, preparing to travel the globe—and the stamps keep on coming.

In 1999, at the age of 29, Catriona's glamorous world collided with the man she'd later move heaven and earth to be with. Her friend invited her to a country party on a farm near Geelong in southern Victoria and it proved to be the best party she'd ever attend. Catriona theatrically recalls the exact moment she locked eyes across the room with a strapping young farmer named James. It wasn't hard to spot Catriona as she wasn't exactly dressed in rural-appropriate attire—she'd turned up wearing a white dress paired with the most beautiful pair of blue suede Manolo Blahnik shoes. James was rugged and had just finished work on the farm, dirt smeared across his face.

'I'd never seen anything like this guy, he'd never seen anything like me and it was lust at first sight.'

While their love story has a happy ending, their journey to be together has been incredibly challenging, especially for Catriona.

With her work and her family cemented deeply in the heart of Sydney and James's on the farm in another state, the pair endured a long-distance relationship until eventually it became clear that someone would have to compromise. At the time, Catriona couldn't bear the thought of leaving her family in Sydney, so at one point she broke things off with James altogether and it was absolutely disastrous. She broke both his heart and her own in the process. One year later, she still hadn't gotten over him and it was clear she'd made a huge mistake. That's when fate came calling in such an unbelievable way, I seriously thought Catriona was joking when she told me this story, so brace yourself.

Catriona was still nursing a broken heart but it was full steam ahead with work, which had kept her mind off things. Twelve months after she broke up with James, she was doing some research for a travel book she was writing when her friend invited her to fly down to Victoria and bunker down at her beach house so she could enjoy a change of scenery and some solitude to write. Coincidentally, her friend's holiday house happened to be just a short drive from James's farm, the ex-boyfriend she just couldn't get off her mind. Catriona took a spontaneous leap of faith and decided to offer the universe one last chance to give her a sign—should she close the chapter on their possible reconciliation for good or reopen it?

'I thought, I'm going to make a vow. I'm going to drive past the back gate of James's farm. If I see him, that'll be a sign.

If I don't see him, that will also be a sign, a sign to finally cut the cord and move on.'

With her cap pulled down firmly over her head for fear of being recognised and feeling like a bit of a stalker, Catriona cased the road running along the back of James's property. Suddenly, her phone rang. It was James. Catriona panicked and thought that he'd spotted her creeping along his boundary but, much to her relief, something far stranger had happened. As Catriona repeatedly yelled 'Hello?' down the phone, with no answer from James, she heard noises in his background and realised it was a pocket dial—James had called her by accident. A few seconds later, James's confused voice was on the other end of the phone; to her excitement, he'd finally picked it up after hearing Catriona's voice booming out of his back pocket. Turns out he'd forgotten to take her off speed dial after they broke up and had accidentally called her when he sat on his phone in the tractor.

> I'm going to drive past the back gate of James's farm. If I see him, that'll be a sign.

'I swear to God, if it hadn't happened to me, I wouldn't believe it was true. The end of the story is I pulled the car over, I sat on the side of the road and we talked on the phone for about an hour. James came to visit me at my friend's beach house the next day.'

Safe to say their reconciliation went well and they promised never to break up again.

Since their chance meeting in 1999, Catriona and James struggled their way through a long-distance relationship for nearly a decade, each adapting to fit into the other's vastly different world. For Catriona, dating James meant weekends spent on the farm doing the most unglamorous of things together. She chipped in where she could, even learning how to deliver lambs, although she admits she'd only pull them out while wearing a pair of her frilly kitchen gloves. As the extroverted, ultra-chic woman she is, it's safe to say that she was less than impressed with some of the farm activities. On the other hand, James, a quieter and more private person, had to endure the limelight alongside Catriona, roaming red carpets and going to public events.

Their two worlds had collided and they were making it work as best as they could. But the moment James proposed to Catriona marked the biggest fork in the road in her life. Getting married and committing to life on the land with him was more permanent and more terrifying than she'd realised. The land was his home and, like many farmers, he would never give up the family property and legacy. The greatest challenge Catriona now faced was that she would have to change her entire lifestyle to be with him and she would have to move away from her family and support network in Sydney and from the Channel Nine studios, the homebase of her livelihood. So, when poor James presented Catriona with the most gorgeous diamond ring and asked her to marry him, she initially told him she'd have to think it over and talk to her family. Her hesitation nearly broke the poor man and infuriated her parents who thought she was being ridiculous. But of course, Catriona knew with every fibre of her being that despite her fears, she and James belonged together, and the next day she put James out of his misery and said yes.

'It was incredibly difficult. And unless somebody compromised, it was never going to come to fruition. I knew that it had to be me.'

They married in 2008, moving into a once-derelict cottage on the farm that they'd spent several years renovating. There wasn't a lot of time for Catriona to soak in rural life as a newlywed, however. Before long, she was back to work, travelling the globe and away for weeks at a time shooting for *Getaway*. Even now, one of the biggest struggles is that while Christmas and January are usually Catriona's time off work to rest and recuperate from a busy year, summer is the busiest time for James on the farm, with things ramping up for a hectic harvesting season.

The first chapter of their life on the land together was busy, exciting and daunting all at the same time. And then the next chapter was the prospect of starting a family together. Catriona told me that before she met James, she didn't think she'd ever have children, but almost immediately after their wedding, Catriona got clucky and was ready to take an even bigger leap, this time into motherhood. While the burning desire to have a family was there, so was the fear of the consequences for her working life.

'I thought, I've found love but I've killed my career,' she says.

Catriona's first son Andrew was born in 2009 and was named after Catriona's late grandfather, her dear nan's husband. Catriona says she was totally unprepared for what awaited her at home on the farm with a newborn. Her mother and nan came down from Sydney to help, but once they left, Catriona was devastated. Motherhood was a huge shock to the system.

'A nurse came to help for the first week then the wheels fell off and I have never missed my mother so much in all my life.'

To ease the isolation she felt as she navigated her way through early motherhood, Catriona decided to join a local mothers' group in the nearest regional town. However, while catching up with her group one day, Catriona noticed that she was being stalked by paparazzi who were vying to get the first exclusive photos of baby Andrew to sell to a magazine. Catriona wasn't having a bar of it. Her talent agent told her either to drive straight to the nearest police station or to take the back roads home and beat the paparazzi there.

'I called James on the way and told him what was happening. His Dad was there, and said he'd get the gun and meet them at the front gate! I said, "For God's sake don't do that or that'll end up as the story!"'

> A nurse came to help for the first week then the wheels fell off and I have never missed my mother so much in all my life.

Even in regional Victoria, Catriona wasn't safe from the public eye and that's something she's navigated throughout her life, shielding her family where possible but also being incredibly accommodating, inviting media into her life at times so she could control the story and raise awareness of issues close to her heart. Motherhood, on the other hand, made her feel completely out of control.

'Oh my God, when I went back to work for the first time after having Andrew, now *that* was a disaster. It just didn't work in the end. It was so difficult.'

Australia's most travelled woman initially had plans for little Andrew to become Australia's most travelled baby. After taking maternity leave, Catriona was excited to take five-month-old Andrew to work with her, thinking she could manage life as a

TV presenter and be a full-time mum. However, while she had the support of her boss, her adventure on the road with her son didn't last long, as the reality of working and travelling with a baby hit home. While Andrew made a couple of appearances on the show in Catriona's arms, flying around the country with him proved to be too difficult and too stressful, with Catriona trying to manage feeding times, nap times and all the demands of an infant while she did her job with a film crew on a tight schedule. Since then, Catriona has juggled work life and home life in more realistic ways, leaning on the support of James and family and friends to create a schedule that works for everyone. She ensures she's never away from home for more than a couple of weeks at a time and jokes that she's spent her career as a FIFO worker. Laughs aside, that is in fact a very accurate description of her working life. Of course, like any parent, it's been hard to be away from home and her children but when I ask her about mum-guilt—don't get Catriona started! She is the master of shedding the blame and guilt that so many of us mums struggle with on a daily basis. Her bluntness on this topic is the pep talk I needed.

'I just accept that mum-guilt never leaves us, it's part of the package. And if you can't hack it, then don't have kids!'

In 2011, after suffering a devastating miscarriage the year before, Catriona welcomed her second son, Charlie. Sadly, Catriona's beloved nan passed away during her pregnancy and never got to meet him. Her death was a devastating blow for Catriona—her nan had been such a big presence in her life and someone Catriona had turned to whenever she needed help or advice. One of the many lessons her nan taught her was to live a life with purpose, or, as Catriona puts it: 'What will be your legacy, and what do you want to be remembered for?' Catriona has leaned into this throughout her life. She's passionate about giving back to the farming industry, a world she's grown to love.

In fact, one of the lightbulb moments Catriona had about how she could support the agriculture industry in a meaningful way came while she was sitting in front of the TV one Sunday afternoon. Catriona proudly admits that over the years she's swapped watching *Keeping up with Kardashians* for farming-related shows like ABC's *Landline*, segments she has treated as homework in a bid to educate and inspire herself on Australia's rural sector. And it was while watching a *Landline* episode on wool that something clicked.

'The story was so bloody boring! In the segment, they mentioned the organisation Australian Wool Innovation and so I just called them the next day. I said, "Listen, I can talk the leg off the chair, everybody knows me, you can send me anywhere. How can I help? Put me to work."'

And so began Catriona's first farming-related job as an ambassador for Australia's wool industry. She shares stories across the supply chain, from farmers right through to clothing designers, putting a spotlight on one of our unique and fast-growing fibre sectors. She might be wool's best PR agent but back on her own sheep farm, Catriona says she's quite comfortable sticking to her ambassador role and steering well clear of any farming jobs, including shearing. She is also happy to share the fact she bypasses several stereotypical 'farmer's wife' duties.

'I cannot cook for shearers to save my life. I just bring them pre-made cake from a packet and they appreciate that much more than my failed attempts at baking!

'The moment that I stopped trying to conform and be what I thought I should be, life took off!'

I have spoken to countless rural mums who, like me, were born and raised in the city and made the move to the country for love. What I've found, and what I've also experienced, is that most of the time, these women find their feet on the land and often, to their surprise, end up enjoying farm life more than their old life. However, Catriona's monumental move to the country is an ongoing compromise for her and she still desperately craves the city at times. And that's what I love about Catriona—her unapologetic honesty about her journey. She didn't talk to me about the incredible life transformation she experienced since living on the land. She doesn't gloat that it's the 'best thing she ever did' (that's my line!). She is real and raw in her personal account of the sacrifices she's made to be where she is today.

> The moment that I stopped trying to conform and be what I thought I should be, life took off!

She's married to the love of her life, with two sons she adores, but it has been far from all sunshine and roses.

'James would be happy if he never left the farm. Too much time on the farm and I go stir crazy, I lose the plot!'

All these years later, she still feels like a 'round peg in a square hole' on the farm but she loves her home and the life she and James have created.

'I adore having this open space. Charlie is learning the trumpet at the moment, and if he wants to go out into the garden and blow that trumpet as loud as possible, he can. So, it's all of these little gifts that a lifestyle like this can give you and that I'm grateful for.'

Catriona approaches life with the most beautiful outlook. Her bubbly personality and positivity are intoxicating and her passion for everything she stands for is infectious. She is, by all accounts, an extrovert and a risk-taker with a thirst for knowledge and a desire to keep learning and growing as a woman, as a wife, as a mother and as one hell of a TV presenter. When we catch up to have a chat about this book, another harvest season is coming to an end for Catriona and James, and she's got a bottle of champagne ready to pop. She's been waiting to celebrate this for months. James's ridiculously long working hours will ease up slightly, which means she'll soon be able enjoy a coffee in bed with him—one of their morning rituals which she adores and has missed.

Speaking of seasons, a new one is about to begin off the farm for Catriona. She's preparing to shoot a record 27th season of *Getaway*. And just when you think she's got all she can handle on her plate, she tells me that she's in the middle of getting her pilot licence and also travelling around regional Australia for a Channel 9 show called *Country House Hunters*, which is inspired by her life and is about finding homes in the country for people seeking a new life away from the city. Catriona is also flying the flag for wool (and in turn supporting her husband's business) by taking on design collaborations with Australian fashion brands such as Iris & Wool and Blue Illusion. 'I love to challenge myself and do things I don't think I can do.

'I want to be like Elle Woods from the *Legally Blonde* movie. You know when she gets a law degree and turns to her ex-boyfriend who thought she wasn't smart enough and says, "What, like it's hard?"!'

By the time season 27 rolls around, Catriona might be flying herself to work. I wouldn't be surprised in the slightest.

# 7

# Julie Mayne: One-woman show

## Dulacca, Queensland

When Julie Mayne told me she was once married to a cowboy, I'll be honest, I thought that sounded pretty cool despite not having a clue what that job description actually entailed. Was he just a farmer who wore a cowboy hat and lived out in the outback mustering cattle on horseback? Not quite. Julie Mayne fell in love with a national rodeo champion; a saddle bronc rider who toured the circuit for a living, getting paid to stay on a bucking horse while fans cheered in the stands.

'That was my life for about seven years. Seven years living in a car and travelling with bareback and bull riders.'

It's safe to say that Julie Mayne has had a wild ride and carpooling with cowboys was just the beginning. Her two children were very young when her rodeo romance crumbled and she suddenly found herself a single mum. She hit restart on her life, took on an entire farm solo and has been an incredible one-woman show in the bush ever since.

Julie grew up on her family's 24,000-hectare farm, which was located between the towns of Tambo and Springsure in central outback Queensland. The property, which Julie's grandmother inherited from her father, was a renovator's delight—a rough and undeveloped block surrounded by gorges, mountains and caves. For the first 30 years of Julie's life, her parents transformed the property, clearing land, installing water bores and putting up boundary fences to increase the cattle-carrying capacity to a few thousand head. For Julie and her younger brother, the farm meant one thing for them as children—freedom. While her parents generally believed that children were meant to be seen and not heard, their style of parenting didn't bother Julie much and it often worked in her favour. Her mum was quite happy for Julie and her brother to disappear out on to the farm in the morning and not come back until dinner time.

'We had this wild childhood! We went out exploring and riding horses and chasing anything that moved. It was excellent.'

Julie completed primary school through School of the Air and Tambo State School before heading to boarding school in

Rockhampton, graduating and returning home to the farm. She stayed there throughout her twenties working for her parents and helping run their cattle operation. But while she adored life there and wanted to call it home forever, she knew the farm would never be hers. From an early age, Julie understood the reality of what it meant to be a female farmer in a generation where males ruled when it came to succession planning. Sadly even today, they often still do. Julie's brother was always destined to take over the farm, no questions asked, meaning Julie would eventually be out on her own. It's something she really struggled to accept, knowing one day she would have to leave, secure some financial independence elsewhere and somehow find her way back to the land—all because of her gender.

'I couldn't understand why I couldn't stay there. That created a lot of resentment in me, growing up with that in the back of my mind. I was just as capable, if not more so. I was just as smart, if not smarter than the boys. So it was really difficult for me to accept that no matter what I did, because I was female, it just wasn't going to happen.'

In 1993 Julie met a man who pulled her far away from the pain surrounding her farming future and into a new world full of adventure. His name was Tom and he was a cowboy who'd grown up on a station in the Northern Territory and was now carving out a rodeo career for himself, competing across the country. Julie met Tom when he came to work on her family's property, filling in for her brother who was away for a few weeks. Tom was tasked with giving Julie a hand with some mustering and other farm jobs for the duration of his stay. While he toured the saddle bronc circuit for most of the year, he was always looking for casual work in between competitions, and he proved to be very handy indeed. While initially he was only supposed to stay for three weeks, the keen cowboy ended up basing himself on Julie's family farm for a couple of years after the two of them hit it off.

Julie and Tom's relationship developed relatively quickly, and after just a few months they set up a side hustle together, using their joint passion for horses to start a business training and breaking in horses for other people. It earned them some decent money on the side when Tom wasn't competing—his rodeo wage was extremely modest. For many months of the year, Julie travelled with Tom across the country to his saddle bronc tournaments, soaking in the excitement and adventure of something so new and so spontaneous, cheering for her man from the stands. For the first couple of years, their rodeo romance was exhilarating, full of socialising in between rides, and long, loud car rides. Julie and Tom carpooled with other cowboys to save money, gallivanting around the country from tournament to tournament. Julie admits that they lived happily on a shoestring, couch-surfing with friends and acquaintances in the towns they toured and living out of a couple of suitcases. Let's face it, being young, in love and child-free makes an adventure like this relatively easy. But two years in and life on the rodeo road had an unexpected twist for Tom and Julie that put their relationship to the ultimate test.

In 1995, Julie fell pregnant with their first child, Ike, a baby boy whom they named after champion American bull rider Ike Sankey. Shortly after unexpectedly finding out they were going to be parents, Tom and Julie got married and decided it was time to spread their wings away from Julie's family farm. They moved into a small, one-bedroom house in the town of Blackall, bought with Julie's savings, and remained relatively unphased about parenthood—Julie continued to ride and break in horses with Tom until she was eight months pregnant. But when she gave birth to her little boy and left the hospital as a doting new mum, it very quickly dawned on her that she wouldn't be having any 'maternity leave', or at least not the traditional kind.

Just eight weeks after giving birth to Ike, at a time when most parents are navigating life with a newborn in the comfort of their own home, managing the intensity of sleep deprivation and trying desperately to slip into some sort of routine, Julie and Tom were doing the exact opposite of 'settling down'. Instead, they were busy figuring out how on earth they were going to fit all the baby gear into one car, a car that they'd be living out of for most of the year because the rodeo circuit was calling and

Tom had to return to work. Julie says she naively assumed that a newborn would fit seamlessly into their busy life on the circuit but the logistical reality of motherhood on the road hit her like a ton of bricks. Julie, baby Ike and Tom squeezed into a white Holden commodore sedan and picked up some passengers on the way, carpooling with two other cowboys who sat shoulder to shoulder with a baby seat next to them in the back.

'Cowboys never have any money, so it's all carpooling. I remember we'd pack up the car, picking up a few competitors along the way, and we'd all put $50 in the ashtray. And that would be the fuel money to get us to the next location.'

So no, Julie wasn't joking when she said she was determined to ensure Ike fitted into their life, regardless of the chaos. And for the first couple of years, things were challenging but relatively happy. Julie and Tom travelled across northern Australia on a tight budget, sticking to their usual frugal arrangements, crashing at friends' houses where they could; and if they didn't have friends to stay with, they'd all chip in for the cheapest hotel possible. No matter where they were, Baby Ike slept in bed with Julie.

. . . we'd all put $50 in the ashtray. And that would be the fuel money to get us to the next location.

Julie's true breaking in to rodeo-mum life came under the bright lights of arenas in Cloncurry, Mount Isa and Darwin. When they arrived at the competition venue, Tom would disappear behind the chutes to join the other competitors, saddle up and prepare for his ride. Julie would juggle Ike's feeds and naps on the go in the noisy showground and, while this sounds like my idea of hell, Julie says she found the nomadic cowboy lifestyle quite easy with one child. Of course, there were tough times. She was extremely sleep-deprived and she lacked any support from family because of how they lived and how often they moved around. But still, things were relatively manageable on the road for the young family and Julie learned to adapt, rid herself of any expectations and enjoy the precious times they had together as a family. The camaraderie and energy of the rodeo world was infectious and she and Tom made lifelong friends on their travels.

'Rodeos are great levellers. You can be a rooster one day and a feather duster the next because you're only as good as your last ride and no one really got a big head. I miss the banter. They were good days.'

Wrangling an energetic toddler at rodeos became slightly more challenging and trickier still when Ike was three years old and Julie and Tom welcomed their little girl Chance. Now they were cramming another baby into the car (ditching one cowboy to make room for another baby seat), and most of the time the four of them had to share a bed wherever they based themselves. Tom would often sleep on the floor in a hotel room or in a swag at someone's house while Julie shared a bed with the kids. It was exhausting and the sleep deprivation was starting to wear Julie down since neither of her children were good sleepers. She began to feel increasingly isolated and under pressure, managing two young children on her own most days and living out of suitcase. She recalls the day she made the decision that enough was enough. Chance was two months old and they'd all travelled to the Blackwater rodeo in the Central Highlands region of Queensland. They arrived at the arena just as it got dark. Tom immediately grabbed his saddle and zipped away and Julie found herself alone again, wrangling an over-tired toddler and a new baby. One was a little tricky, but two was a logistical nightmare.

'I remember getting the pram out and negotiating the crowds, and then I thought, I need to go to the toilet. I took the pram into a public toilet and I had to bring a torch because the lights weren't working, and I just thought, nah, I can't do this anymore, this is just not me. So I put my foot down.'

After that night, Julie decided it was time for her to stay at home with the kids for some peace and normality. Tom continued to travel and compete for the next couple of years, returning home every few weeks or months. In between tournaments, he and Julie continued to break horses in for some extra income but sadly their marriage was slowly crumbling. Julie and Tom drifted apart and eventually ended their seven-year marriage when Chance was two years old and Ike was five. Their separation was messy and painful, and Julie clearly recalls the day Tom left the farm for good.

'I remember crying solidly for three weeks and then wondering what I was going to do. I had two children to look after on my own. It was really difficult.'

Fortunately, Julie is a savvy businesswoman and fiercely independent, and she had wisely prepared for tough times in the years prior to her marriage breakdown. Tom's rodeo pay cheques were only ever enough to get them all from one tournament to the next. Once they became parents Julie had stepped up to take control and had bought the one-bedroom house in Blackall with her own money. She'd saved up her earnings from working on her parents' farm over the years and was able to buy the house in Blackall when she was pregnant with Ike. It had cost her $11,000 and was run down to say the least, full of shotgun pellet holes and in desperate need of a makeover. Over time, Julie painted it inside and out and in her words 'bodged' it all up so she could one day flip it. After her daughter Chance was born, she sold that house for $25,000 and bought another home, this one was slightly bigger. She painted it, polished the floorboards and did some landscaping before selling it for $40,000. Over the years, she'd also purchased a small 20-hectare block of land in Blackall, had amassed 45 cows and had plans to convert the land to a caravan park one day, but she never got the chance. After her marriage breakdown, with only the small block to her name, Julie was able to sell the property, pocket some savings and use the rest to buy herself a small, dated truck. Julie was preparing to be a one-woman show, and the show was about to begin.

As she faced life as a single mum, Julie found work as a caretaker on several farms in the Blackall region. She did everything from checking water, fencing, checking and moving cattle and the odd repair job, using the truck she'd bought to transport cattle around the region for other farmers. It was the perfect set-up for Julie as it kept her financially secure and connected to the land. She sent her son to a local school and took her three-year-old daughter to work with her each day. The farming skills Julie had learned from her father as she grew up on her family's property ultimately gave her the independence and freedom she craved. After working for twelve months around the region, Julie was offered a job that she didn't see coming. Her parents had purchased another property at Dulacca in Queensland, 550 kilometres from the family farm, and they offered her the position of caretaker.

'It's as if all of a sudden they realised that other people could see value in their daughter, so then they asked me to come on board and look after their new farm for them. It was a bit of a shock. I didn't think I'd ever be given that kind of opportunity.'

The job offer was a bittersweet moment for Julie and a big fork in the road in her journey. After the hurt she had felt following her parent's succession planning decision involving her brother years earlier, part of Julie didn't want to accept their invitation to manage the new farm. On the flip side, however, it offered Julie an amazing opportunity to start afresh, to have some long-term security and a permanent home for her and her children in the bush. But still, Julie felt she had to swallow some pride before accepting her parents' offer.

'It was really overwhelming. I was proud and independent and I felt like a bit of a failure. After everything I'd been through, I thought, oh my God, I'm back working for my family.'

In 2004, Julie and her two children moved six hours south-east of Blackall to their new home at Dulacca, which had a population of just over 100. Julie took on Coolamon, the 1200-hectare property that her parents initially purchased as a drought-relief block, but that Julie has transformed into much more over the years. Julie didn't just wear a lot of hats when she moved there, she wore all the hats. When she drove through the gates of Coolamon for the first time, she became farm manager, builder, repairwoman, contractor and financial manager all at once, and there was a hell of a lot of work to be done. Over the following few years, she transformed the property into a business she could manage on her own, with her two little helpers by her side. She built her own one-woman cattle yards, which to this day enable her to do most of the cattle work solo. She fenced the property in a way that made it easier for her to muster, she installed a water system for cattle and she took on all the maintenance work. Ike and Chance watched on, unaware of just how accomplished their mum was. When her children were still very little and it was too dangerous for them to be involved in some of the farm jobs, Julie had to improvise. She'd bribe them with snacks, set up their colouring-in books and do anything to get them to sit still so she could get to work.

'If I did cattle work, I would take my car down to the yards, put them in the car, and I'd say, "Whatever you do, don't get out of the car. If you need me, just beep the horn!"'

As they got older, Ike and Chance were allowed out of the car and into the cattle yards with Julie to give her a much-needed helping hand. They learned the ropes very quickly—documenting animal weights and tag numbers and helping their mum muster. They saw the very best and the very worst of life on the land, helping Julie bring new life into the world when their calves were born each year, but also confronting the reality of death, sometimes by Julie's side, helping her if she had to put an animal down.

If I did cattle work, I would take my car down
to the yards, put them in the car, and I'd say,
'Whatever you do, don't get out of the car.
If you need me, just beep the horn!'

When it came to their schooling, the closest option was at Drillham, 20 kilometres away. It was a one-teacher town and Julie's kids attended their primary school there, supported by a wonderful teacher who managed a classroom of 22 children, all different ages. Given the size of the school and its remote location, most co-curricular activities required a fair bit of travel. To ensure Ike and Chance didn't miss out on things like carnivals or sports events which required a day trip or even overnight trips on occasion, Julie had to get creative. Being away from the farm for extended periods of time is difficult for most farmers, but for Julie it was near impossible; she couldn't just take a day off given she had no employees to help or manage the farm while she was gone. When you have animals that need checking, or water that needs fixing so they can drink, you can't just jump in the car and abandon ship at the drop of a hat. So there were many occasions where Julie, Ike and Chance would be up until late at night, all chipping in to get the farm jobs done so they could hit the road in the morning and drive to wherever they needed to be.

There were also many times when school took a back seat and family time and farm time were the priorities. If Julie had to venture out of town in her truck to pick up or drop off cattle, then she'd often pull the kids out of school so they could come with her. Sometimes, these trips were a logistical necessity; at other times, it was purely because the three of them were a tight-knit trio and Julie adored spending as much time with them as possible.

'They came everywhere with me. I wasn't shy about taking them out of school. I just thought, these are the times that they'll remember, falling asleep in the truck and getting home at 2 am with Mum.'

Despite all the obstacles Julie faced as a young single mum on the land, nothing much has rattled her over all these years. Becoming a mother has been the greatest gift of her life and she has embraced the ups and the downs wholeheartedly. What she has struggled with the most is the crippling isolation she felt when her children were in their late teens, preparing to leave the nest. Ike graduated from high school and left home to begin work at the same time as Chance, who was about to begin Year 10 and had been awarded a scholarship, was preparing to leave home to attend boarding school in Toowoomba. For the first time, Julie found herself completely alone on the farm.

'That was a very empty time for me. I had to find my purpose again. All of a sudden, they were gone. They were very independent people and I was left with a big void.'

Julie struggled to find ways to fill that void for several years after her children left home. On the business side of things, times were tough as her region was in the grip of a seven-year drought. The extra pressure on Julie was intense as she struggled to keep things afloat, borrowing money to trade cattle, picking up extra work carting stock around in the region in her truck and trying desperately to avoid selling her own breeding herd, which had grown over the years to 300 head. Eventually, in 2015 things had become so tough that Julie craved a way to escape the harsh reality of drought. For her own mental wellbeing, she wanted to shift her energy to something she could control. Julie has always been exceptional with her hands—she's a great builder, whether it's welding or fencing, and she's always had a creative side. As a child, she'd make figurines and animals out of scrap wire that she found lying around her family's farm. One day, walking around her property during the drought, feeling a bit down, she started noticing all the unused metal scraps on her own property and had an idea.

> That was a very empty time for me. I had to find my purpose again. All of a sudden, they were gone.

Julie's creative quest resulted in her building spectacular sculptures made from the scrap metal she found around the station. It started as a hobby, but her side hustle has since grown into a thriving business. She has been commissioned to weld giant spheres made from old plough discs, cultivator feet or horseshoes, so she can diversify her income during the dry times, but this creative outlet has also been a critical part of her emotional wellbeing.

'It was a really important tool for my mental health and I don't know what I would have done without it. Going out on the farm and looking at your hungry cattle every day was just heartbreaking.'

In November 2021, the eight-year drought finally broke and the rain came thick and fast, bucketing for weeks. The reprieve came just in time for Julie, who was otherwise facing the prospect of selling all her cattle.

'It makes me cry, actually, when it rains. It's just so overwhelming. It's been eight years of looking at dirt and scrimping and saving and adjusting and leasing land.'

The weather gods finally delivered the goods, and when Julie and I catch up in mid-2022, her farm is thriving, luscious grass is growing and the cattle prices are high, which makes for one very happy farmer! And while Julie is keeping very busy with a thumping season on farm, off the farm she has also found her purpose in the broader agriculture industry as an advocate for rural and regional women. She's the president of the Queensland Rural, Regional and Remote Women's Network, a not-for-profit organisation that celebrates and connects women across the state, providing leadership and networking opportunities in agriculture. Julie has harnessed more than 30 years of her experience as a farmer, businesswoman and single mum to become a highly respected role model and mentor for rural women. But she is quick to point out that her greatest role models are the women who have shaped the landscape before her.

'All women associated with the land are remarkable: my neighbours, my friends, my associates . . . Every day they are juggling family, business, community, industry requirements and climate issues. And, they do all this with grace and integrity, and a 'just get on with it' attitude. They are my inspiration.'

Ike and Chance are now in their twenties. Ike travels wherever he is needed across the country as a specialist operator and supervisor in the construction/logistics (oil, gas, transport and coal) industry, and Chance has recently finished her fifth year of medicine. There's no doubt Julie longs for them to return to the land one day, although there's no knowing if they'll ever come home given the paths each has taken since leaving school. However, if either of them decides to pursue a future in farming, the land, their land, will be waiting, and so will Julie.

'Having children and being a rural mother has taught me. It's the best education anyone can have. It's taught me to be selfless and it's enabled me to find strength I never knew I had.'

# 8

# Keelen Mailman: Against all the odds

## Mount Tabor, Queensland

Keelen Mailman is a proud Bidjara woman and a force to be reckoned with. She lives at Mount Tabor, a 73,000-hectare cattle station near Augathella in western Queensland—land that belongs to her people and land she's been managing for the past 25 years after becoming the first Aboriginal woman in Australia to run a commercial cattle property. Over the past few decades, Keelen has achieved so much for herself and her ancestors. She's a fierce advocate for traditional owners and went to extreme lengths to achieve her lifelong goal of having the remains of the Bidjara people returned to their country.

Keelen has spent her life fighting, and she acknowledges that she's done too much of it. For all the highs in recent years, she's also suffered through incredible lows and has triumphed against all the odds. She's survived poverty, racism, domestic violence and childhood abuse. Now, she's a doting mother and a grandmother but there have been times throughout her life when she thought she had no future.

'One day, I drove the car straight into the telephone pole because I thought I just wanted to end my life, I just don't want this anymore. If this is what I've got to live with and this is all I deserve, I might as well not be here. And of course, I ended up surviving, thankfully.'

Keelen was born in 1966 in Clermont in western Queensland but her early years were spent with her family on the fringes of Augathella at the Yumba, an Aboriginal camp. She grew up in a tin hut with dirt floors, which she lived in with her grandparents, mother, brothers and sisters. It was a tight squeeze and an even tighter-knit community. Just one shared tap provided water to more than a dozen families. Throughout her childhood, Keelen's respect and connection to her culture grew as she listened intently to all the Dreamtime stories her mother shared. She hated school and longed to be home with her family where she learned things she could never learn in a classroom.

'My mum was very strict about us knowing our traditional land and how to live off the land with our cultural fruits, foods and medicines if we were ever stuck. So that was a big part of my life.'

Keelen and her siblings lived an incredible bush life, sourcing honey from native bees, fishing for yabbies, finding buried eggs from thuckange (sand goanna) and hunting porcupine (echidna)—a skill Keelen prided herself on because from a young age she was able to track, kill, clean and cook the prickly animal, serving it up with homemade damper for a family feast. Keelen's mother wanted to ensure her children could survive on their own if they ever needed to, and Keelen even recalls being taught how to strip bark off a bottle tree to access water and its soft, edible inner bark. Keelen has fond memories of the Yumba and her confidence and independence grew as her connection to her culture deepened. But she had no idea just how much she'd come to rely on her strength and independence in the years to come.

> My mum was very strict about us knowing our traditional land and how to live off the land with our cultural fruits, foods and medicines if we were ever stuck . . .

When Keelen was around ten years old, she and her family moved to the town of Charters Towers where her stepfather had family. She describes that time as a sheer nightmare because she and her siblings were neglected and barely fed at times, while her mother battled alcoholism and was the victim of domestic violence. At one point, Keelen's mum was beaten so badly by her partner when she was pregnant that she delivered a stillborn baby. After that loss, Keelen's mother began drinking heavily again and was on a downward spiral. Finding a lost wallet at a pub one night, her mum finally had the money to buy Keelen and her siblings a train ticket out of there and they headed back home to Augathella. This time, they moved into a house, not the Yumba. Heartbreakingly, for the next couple of years, Keelen was repeatedly sexually abused by one of her uncles who told her if she reported him, no one would believe her and she'd be taken away. But by the time Keelen had reached the age of twelve, she fought back, knowing deep down that it was wrong and the abuse needed to stop. After confronting him one day and telling him she'd report him, he beat her to a pulp, but she kept fighting back until eventually he let her go and fled. He didn't come back to town until years later when he tried to offer Keelen money and to apologise but she rejected any communication with him. It was a living nightmare at times for Keelen who had to find incredible strength at such a young age and her strength was about to be tested to its limits again because later that year, her mother suffered a massive stroke at the age of just 38. Keelen and her brothers and sisters found her slumped in a chair one afternoon, her eyes were open but she didn't blink or respond to anything.

'That was the day when our whole world fell apart. She was taken to hospital and she was in a coma for six months. We didn't know if she'd ever come back.'

Keelen and her siblings were suddenly alone at home and without any support or anyone to look after them for several days before one of their aunts came from Charleville to help after hearing what had happened. She brought her own children with her and looked after them all. Eventually, Keelen's mum was finally discharged from hospital and was allowed to come home, although she was still bedridden for some time after that. The reality of her recovery was a cruel shock for her kids.

'I can remember quite clearly in my memory running through the doors of the hospital because we were so happy that our mum was back and she'd come back and we could see her again and then the fear of God on her face because she didn't know who we were and what we wanted. So, we had to teach her that she owned us, we were her children and she was our mum. So, it was quite a sad and traumatic time for us.'

When her mother was home, there were eleven of them living in the same house and everyone had to share the load of looking after the younger children. Eventually, their aunty packed up and left them, heading back to Charleville with her children, leaving Keelen, along with her older brother and sister, to take over the role of mother, forced to care for their own mum as well as look after their younger siblings. It was an incredibly difficult time for Keelen who was just a child herself when she was entrusted with an adult level of responsibility. As her recovery dragged on, her mum started drinking again and in their late teens, Keelen's older brother and older sister both left town to start their lives elsewhere; the pressure was too much. From there, it was just Keelen alone with her four younger siblings to care for—and a mother who was incapable of caring for anyone. Her younger brothers and sisters were in primary school in Augathella while Keelen was in high school in Charleville, an hour away by bus. Eventually the stress and responsibility of having to cook, clean and care for everyone became too much for Keelen; she was exhausted. When she started skipping school more regularly, others started to notice and she became terrified when a former policeman saw her in town and warned her that she and her siblings could all be taken away. After that conversation, Keelen went back to her house and didn't leave it for twelve months.

'I went into hiding and did not leave that house for a year. I told my younger brothers and sisters not to tell anyone that their sister was there or they'd come and take us all. We were pretty much half-starving because we didn't have very much of anything.'

The gas was cut off and Keelen used a wood stove downstairs to boil hot water and cook their food. She also did the handwashing late at night before hanging it out so that nobody could see she was in the house. She was paranoid. Life became slightly easier when she was alerted to the fact that during the course of that year, all the mail Keelen had been filing away in a drawer without opening was actually pension money for her bedridden mother. Straight away, she started forging her mum's signature, paying the bills and finally being able to afford more groceries so they could all survive more comfortably. But after her first stroke, Keelen's mother was never the same and she had a series of smaller strokes that eventually led to her being put in the care of a nursing home.

Keelen was seventeen years old (or so she thought) when two extraordinary things happened to her. Firstly, she fell in love with a country boy called Ronnie who was doing some work mustering at nearby properties. She very quickly fell pregnant and had her first baby that same year, a son called Allan. Soon after, she went to get her learner driver's licence but when she was told she needed to get a copy of her birth certificate as she had no other ID, her world was sent into a spin. When she opened the mail and looked at the certificate, nothing made sense. You see, up until this moment, Keelen thought her name was 'Kayleen'—that's what her mum had called her, that's what everyone knew her as back then. She also thought she was born in 1965, meaning at the time of applying for her licence, she was seventeen years old. But staring back at her was information that stated her birth name was in fact Keelen, and her date of birth was 29 November 1966, not 1965. According to her birth certificate, she was one year younger than she thought, with a different name.

'I thought holy shit, this isn't me, they've got this all wrong. I got back in touch with the office and said you've got the wrong person. Well, it wasn't a mistake!'

Keelen's mother burst out laughing when she was asked about the mix-up, saying she had no idea she'd jotted down a different name and the wrong year of birth all those years ago. It was an innocent and bizarre mistake that Keelen forgave. Instantly, she'd gained a year of youth, meaning she was just sixteen years old when she had her baby Allan, not seventeen as she thought. And with her birth certificate and all future official documents needing to refer to her birth name Keelen, she decided to embrace that name. The twists and turns of Keelen's life are quite extraordinary, and at this point in our conversation, I realise she's only just getting started!

I thought holy shit, this isn't me, they've got this all wrong . . . Well, it wasn't a mistake!

Keelen says she savoured early motherhood and was an adoring mum to Allan. But slowly, the relationship with her partner crumbled and soon she found herself as a single mum struggling to make ends meet. But in her quest for lifelong love, it wasn't long before she met another man called Paul, a rodeo rider who swept her off her feet and with whom she had a daughter, called Kristy. She and Paul eventually moved to Brisbane to give city life a go. For Keelen, the racism she endured in the rural west was difficult to handle and she thought a fresh start in the big smoke was the right thing to do, but a few years later her relationship with Paul came to a bitter end and Keelen was once again on her own—only this time, with two children. But she hadn't given up on love, and it would find her again, but the third time around it wouldn't just be her heart that was broken.

'I was single for a while and that's when I met Mike (not his real name). And everything was sort of in the honeymoon phase and hunky-dory happiness, until he moved in and then the whole of my life changed after around fifteen-odd months of him living there.'

Over time, Keelen realised the man she loved was not who she thought he was. Mike changed and became increasingly violent towards her. His behaviour escalated to the point where Keelen was regularly beaten, sexually assaulted a number of times and, at one point, she recalls Mike chasing her with an axe. This relationship rocked Keelen to her core and shattered her self-confidence. She was scared not only for her own life but for the lives of her two young children and she started to suffer from debilitating anxiety to the point where she couldn't swallow her food and would choke on it. She also felt incredible shame for the treatment she'd endured for so long and even considered taking her own life. But after purposely crashing her car into a pole while Mike was sitting beside her and walking away with just whiplash, she had a wake-up call and decided enough was enough.

'I sat there in that car for those few minutes with him once again giving me a couple more hits. I reflected on my children that I loved more than anything and I thought, *What are you doing?* I'm a big believer in my ancestors and I believe that the strength came from them that particular day.'

Keelen got a domestic violence order against Mike, reported injuries to her doctor and prepared to mount a case against him, but, in the meantime, he fled, stealing most of her belongings in the process. Keelen was left broke, but she was finally free and her kids were safe.

What happened next in Keelen's life is what she refers to as her spiritual calling. After surviving horrific abuse and struggling to support her children on her own, she was offered a very special opportunity. At a time when she was already thinking of going back home to Augathella and taking her children back to her cultural roots, she got a call. A friend asked her if she wanted a few weeks of work in nearby Adavale doing some cultural monitoring, essentially identifying cultural sites and working to protect them. Keelen immediately said yes and, over those few weeks assisting with that project, she did some incredibly special work, including finding ancient tools, artifacts and rock engravings. She felt a calling back to country and knew home is where she needed to be. By this time, Keelen's children were teenagers and Keelen admits that initially they weren't keen on moving back to Augathella, but they warmed up to the idea.

Keelen got a job working with Community Development Employment Projects, the work-for-the-dole program. At first, she did lawn mowing around town, then, soon after, she scored a traineeship as a librarian's aid. But she never completed the twelve-month program because once again country called and a highly respected elder and local leader in the community approached Keelen with a job opportunity that would change her life forever.

'He said, "How would you like to manage Mount Tabor Station for our people?"'

Mount Tabor is a 73,000-hectare cattle property on traditional country two hours out of Augathella on mostly dirt roads. It was purchased by the Indigenous Land Corporation in 1997 because of its cultural significance to the Bidjara people, with many cultural artifacts, burial sites and rock art and stencilling sites scattered across the property. Keelen took the job in 1998 and has been managing the property ever since.

He said, 'How would you like to manage
Mount Tabor Station for our people?'

'Bringing my children out into no-man's land, they said to me, "Mum, you've brought us that far out in the middle of whoop whoop, how much further do you want to take us?"'

They didn't have access to free-to-air TV, so Keelen would ask the local store to send them a couple of movies on cassette tape each week so they had something to watch. Providing her children with an education was a huge labour of love for Keelen who, despite not having finished school herself, helped homeschool her daughter Kristy via distance education while managing the homestead and the cultural sites across the property. A couple of years into her adventure on Mount Tabor, Keelen had another child, a baby girl called Charlee, with her partner David whom she stayed with for ten years before they parted ways and he moved from the station. While Keelen says she's felt enormous judgement from others regarding her personal relationships, she fiercely defends herself, even though she shouldn't have to.

'A lot of people might look and think, "Crikey, she's had three different kids to three different fellows." Well, my answer to that and to those women and people out there who are judgemental is, "Why should I stay in a relationship if it wasn't working and I wasn't happy?" Because then that impacts your child. You deserve to have love and happiness and I moved on and thought that I had that all over again and that didn't work out.'

Keelen loves her job, which has evolved over the years, along with her home life. At one point, her household grew from being home to her three children to being home to eight children when sadly Keelen became aware that her sister was struggling to care for her own children and was also suffering from horrific domestic violence. To protect her sister's children, Keelen stepped in and fought in court to get guardianship of her four nieces and a nephew and brought them out to Mount Tabor station. At that time, Keelen was caring for six children under the age of fifteen.

'Cooking, cleaning and then distance education was pretty hard for me because I didn't have a lot of education myself and all the new stuff. And then I felt that I was failing the kids, so I just had to keep pulling strength from within all the time. I thought, I'm giving them the best that I can and at least I'm giving them love and a home where they're happy and safe.'

A lot of people didn't think Keelen would last the distance in the vast outback of Mount Tabor. The elder who had given her the job even copped flak with people saying there was no way a young single mum could do the 'job of a bloke' out there. Some of the old Bidjara men in town even put bets down that she wouldn't last. Well, who's laughing now? The property was run down when Keelen took over—there was overgrown grass, no water and ageing infrastructure. Her son Allan got a job working alongside his mum and together they fixed the fences and tidied the property up. It was a tough first few years and Keelen had limited tools to work with, being given just a car, wire for fencing, one pair of pliers, one shovel, a crowbar and a small chainsaw. She worked seven days a week for around $165 a week, and finally found some additional financial support from the government to assist her with raising the children but it was still difficult at times to make ends meet. Keelen learned to make her own bullets by hand and would go out hunting and skinning kangaroos for some extra money. It was important to her that she send the children to high school in Toowoomba, which she was able to do. When her role as a mother started to slow down, her kids finishing high school and becoming more and more independent, Keelen's career started to accelerate.

Keelen was the person who fought to have 100 per cent ownership of Mount Tabor Station and have it returned to the Bidjara people. In 2016, the property was handed over to the Goorathuntha Traditional Owners Limited (GTOL), a monumental occasion which fell on Keelen's 50th birthday. GTOL kept Keelen on as the property's manager and, together with the Bidjara people, Keelen has been working hard for many years to get approval for a healing and rehabilitation station to be established on the station to help at-risk Indigenous youth—a project that would also help generate more funds for the Mount Tabor business. But Keelen's most extraordinary mission to date occurred several years earlier and is deeply personal and close to her heart. Throughout her childhood, Keelen heard her family talk about some of the ancestral remains of the Bidjara people that were stolen by collectors in the twenties, apparently in the name of research. The rare bark coffins contained the bones of Bidjara people—a woman, three men and a child—who had been placed in traditional burial locations but whose remains were extracted, moved around and, years later, placed in the Queensland Museum.

'To have them taken away from their final resting place: I mean, I don't think anyone in the country would like somebody going into a cemetery and digging up the remains and taking them. And listening to the heartache from my mum and my aunty and elders, I thought, well, you know what, we've got to bring them home.'

Determined, Keelen entered into negotiations that lasted seven years and eventually she won the fight, which marked perhaps one of the biggest moments of her life. In 2012, the museum returned the ancestral remains to the Bidjara people. During the floods that year, Keelen kept the remains safe in her home until it was suitable to return them out on country.

The ancestral bones were then transferred by Keelen and other Bidjara people to new coffins made from bark from the buderoo tree and their new burial location is a closely guarded secret. The milestone moment prompted enormous celebrations and ceremonies by the local Bidjara people and Keelen talks about this in her memoir, *The Power of Bones*.

'It was an extraordinary spiritual journey that I took with my ancestors and having them in the house with me for six months before I got to place them back out on traditional country was so powerful and special. I'll remember that until the day I die.'

Keelen Mailman has overcome extraordinary hurdles throughout her life, and she's been rightly recognised as a trailblazing woman on several occasions. In 2007, she was a Queensland finalist in the Australian of the Year awards; in 2009, she was selected for the Australian Rural Leadership program; and in 2016, she was honoured by winning both state and national Bernados Mother of the Year. In 2021, Keelen was awarded the Order of Australia for her commitment and contribution to her local community and her culture, a passion which is undeniable. Keelen still calls Mount Tabor Station home, caring for the land, her people and their deep-rooted culture that spans thousands of years on their land. Looking back at what she's endured and the many more predictable paths her life could have taken if it weren't for the hardship she has experienced, what Keelen has achieved single-handedly throughout her life is nothing short of astonishing.

'I'm quite proud of the woman that I've become. I reckon I've made my mum and my old ancestors and my family proud.'

# 9

# Sabrina Davis: The Black Summer

## Kangaroo Island, South Australia

When smoke started choking the air and flames drew closer to Sabrina's property, she remained calm. She'd prepared for this. She loaded her two children into the car with an overnight bag for them all, as well as their emergency box, which contained their passports, ID, birth certificates and insurance papers. And as she drove out of her farm, leaving her husband behind to defend their home, it never crossed her mind that she'd regret what she packed that day. It was all unimportant, given what was about to happen.

As fire engulfed their community, Sabrina told her five-year-old daughter and seven-year-old son that they were going away for a short, two-day sleepover at their grandparents and would return home soon. Less than six hours later, their farm was incinerated as the raging Black Summer fires tore through Kangaroo Island, and in an instant Sabrina and her family had no home to return to.

'After hours of no communication and not knowing if he was alive, Ben finally called to tell me we'd lost everything. All I could think was: how am I going to tell the children?'

Sabrina's story begins a very long way from Kangaroo Island. She was born and raised in a small village of 500 people just outside a town called Magdeburg in Germany, south-west of Berlin. She grew up on one side of the Berlin Wall, a guarded concrete barrier with barbed wire that physically and ideologically divided the country from 1961 to 1989 and became a fixture in the Cold War landscape. While Sabrina was too young to understand the political unrest that had consumed her country, she remembers the impact that the concrete divide had on her family. She had relatives she didn't see or even meet for years because they weren't allowed to travel from the other side of the wall. Her grandmother would line up for hours just to buy fruits such as bananas, which were considered 'exotic' and only available to purchase once a year. Things we now take for granted like cars and telephones simply weren't accessible. It's incredible to think that this is the world Sabrina was living in only 35 years ago. But finally, on 9 November

1989, it was announced that the Wall would come down, and its celebrated demise marked the beginning of the end of communism in Eastern and Central Europe. Sabrina was nearly seven years old when the borders finally opened and, almost immediately, life changed for the better.

'Suddenly there were cars! We also had access to all these different fruits and foods and Barbie dolls! I'd heard about them, but I'd never seen one. Eventually my family and I started to go on holidays too. It was crazy.'

Sabrina has had a love for travelling and new experiences ever since that wall came down. Her family eventually moved to the city of Munich and after studying public relations, marketing and communications at university, Sabrina went on to work in a glamorous job in PR for five years. In 2008 she was ready for a new adventure and applied for an Australian working holiday visa, resigned from her job, packed a suitcase and headed Down Under. Little did she know that soon she'd call a unique part of Australia home.

When Sabrina touched down in Sydney on a mild spring morning, she did what many backpackers do and checked into a hostel in the city to plan her next move. Over the weeks that followed, she ticked all the usual suspects off her Sydney tourist bucket list before buying a campervan and heading off to explore the rest of the country. Over the next six months, she travelled around Australia, working on a farm near Tamworth and doing some promotional work on the Gold Coast before landing a short stint at a PR firm in Melbourne. After that, she decided to get off the beaten track and hit the road along the south coast, making her way through Victoria, South Australia and over to Western Australia before ending up in Broome, where the wet season stopped her in her tracks. She'd planned on heading over to Darwin to explore the Northern Territory but she was told by locals that she wasn't at all prepared for the conditions that lay ahead and should turn back.

'I had no idea and didn't really understand what the wet season meant. But my vehicle was not equipped to make that journey. So, I ended up going back to Perth to sell the van and decided to go WWOOFing; basically, volunteering as a farm worker on organic farms in return for board and lodging.'

Unsure of where to head next on her adventure, Sabrina met a German girl who recommended she visit idyllic Kangaroo Island. As Australia's third largest island, it spans 155 kilometres in length, outlined by raw and rugged coastline and impeccably clear waters, and has a population of just over 4000 people. Agriculture is still its most significant industry and it has a thriving sheep and wool sector. So, when Sabrina saw a volunteering opportunity advertised with a local beekeeper who boasted they were only 500 metres from the beach, she didn't need any convincing. She called up the host who had listed the position and was immediately offered a place and told a bed would be available for her in three days' time. The next day, Sabrina booked her plane tickets and headed to the island to begin working for the man who one day would become her brother-in-law.

Sabrina remembers the moment she locked eyes with this man's brother, Ben; it was her first day on the island and Ben had come to visit his brother. Ben and Sabrina were instantly drawn to each other and ended up spending the entire afternoon talking and getting to know each other. Sabrina was one of several international farm workers helping on the property at the time but she was the only one who spoke English well enough to communicate with him in-depth. Within minutes she had Ben's undivided attention. Their love story blossomed very quickly and they started seeing each other as much as they could in between their responsibilities. They dated for a few months before travelling around half of Australia together in a campervan and finally finishing the adventure that Sabrina had serendipitously been prevented from completing months earlier. Shortly after they arrived back on Kangaroo Island, Ben, who lived on the family's sheep farm half an hour from where Sabrina was working, asked her to move in with him.

'Life on the island was a bit of a shock to the system in general because I came from a PR, red-carpet, glitz-and-glamour life in Germany, and there's nothing glamorous about living on a farm, especially not a sheep farm on Kangaroo Island!'

While their relationship grew stronger, so did Sabrina's fondness for her new, unglamorous life. However, her time was fast running out because her one-year working holiday visa was nearing its expiry date. Eventually, the time came for her to return home to Germany and she was heartbroken to leave Ben and the farm life they'd started to create together. Sabrina returned to her PR job in Munich and tried to settle back into life at home, but Australia, and Ben, had changed her forever. It was actually her mother, who saw how miserable her daughter was and who made the decision just five weeks later to buy her daughter a one-way ticket to Australia, encouraging her to follow her heart. Sabrina had applied for a second 12-month working visa some months prior and was over the moon when it was approved in time for her flight out of Germany. She returned to Kangaroo Island and straight into the arms of Ben, the cute Aussie farmer who, she was beginning to realise, was much more than just a holiday fling.

Sabrina and Ben settled into life together on his farm on the western end of Kangaroo Island, surrounded by conservation park and plantations. Ben was busy with their 500 head of sheep and beekeeping, while Sabrina found work at a hotel on the island. A couple of years later, the pair got engaged and married within a few months, with suddenly even more news on the horizon.

Sabrina fell pregnant with their first child, a boy they named Jordan, but his entrance into the world and Sabrina's transition to motherhood proved to be one of the toughest times of her life. At 34 weeks pregnant, she fell at work and, in an effort to protect her baby, stuck her arm out to soften the fall, breaking her wrist in the process. A few weeks later when she went into labour, still wearing a wrist brace, she was told it was likely she wouldn't be able to pick up her newborn son after he was born. However, her broken wrist would soon prove to be the least of everyone's concerns, as Sabrina was soon fighting for her life. After a gruelling, 24-hour labour, Sabrina suffered a fourth-degree tear and catastrophic blood loss. She was flown off the island by the Royal Flying Doctor Service and taken to Flinders Hospital in Adelaide for emergency surgery and several blood transfusions.

'Everyone else around me was screaming but I was just really calm because at that point I felt like there was nothing I could do. I remember feeling really, really cold. I remember seeing a light and I just knew my life was at risk.'

Sabrina doesn't remember much of this part at all, but her husband later told her that at one point she begged him to look after their newborn son when she was gone and told him to say goodbye to her loved ones for her because she was sure she was going to die. It was a heart-stopping few hours for everyone, including Sabrina's mother who was visiting from Germany at the time. Preparing to meet her first grandchild, she was instead faced with the prospect of losing her daughter.

Everyone else around me was screaming but I was just really calm because at that point I felt like there was nothing I could do . . .

Doctors saved Sabrina's life, and little Jordan, who was flown to Adelaide with her and new-dad Ben, was thankfully fighting fit. But while her birth emergency was over, Sabrina's recovery dragged on for a long time after she was discharged from hospital. She was bed-bound for three months after she returned to the farm, and she was unable to do anything but feed her baby between resting and sleeping. She was on countless pills and medications to help her heal and cope with the pain, and over this difficult time she fell into the depths of postnatal depression. She was struggling to cope as a new mum at the same time as trying to process the birth trauma she'd suffered, while living on a remote property more than 100 kilometres away from Ben's closest relatives. Sabrina eventually sought professional help from a counsellor and, after flying to Germany and staying with her family for six weeks for some extra support, she finally started to feel a little bit like herself again. Contrary to what everyone expected after all this, it wasn't long before she felt ready to try for another baby.

Two year later, Sabrina and Ben were blessed with their daughter Kerily, whose birth was a planned C-section. Everything went to plan and thankfully Sabrina found her recovery much easier this time. Unlike her experience with her son, she was able to soak up the early newborn months with her daughter—with an energetic toddler by her side, of course!

'My doctor actually couldn't believe it when I told him I was pregnant again. He said, "I didn't think I would see you for another eight years!"'

As for so many rural families, accessing childcare services when her children were little wasn't an option for Sabrina. The nearest day care centre on the island was 100 kilometres away and, although she would have loved the additional support on the difficult days, she thrived on being a full-time mum until both her children started school. In 2018, she found herself working again when her neighbour became a quadriplegic after a horrific farming accident. He'd also been managing an accommodation business on his property and, as he was unable to work anymore, Sabrina—who will go to great lengths to help people as you'll soon discover—stepped in.

Sabrina volunteered to manage her neighbour's business to help him keep things afloat and she did this seven days a week for more than eighteen months. At the time, her son had started school in the nearest town while her daughter, who was just four years old, accompanied her to work every day. While Sabrina managed reception, took bookings, greeted tourists, managed staff and often had to assist with the cleaning of the rooms, her little girl was right by her side. But Sabrina's busy work schedule and being on-call 24/7 soon took its toll emotionally as she realised what she really craved was to spend more time with her children, especially while they were so young. So, just before the school Christmas holidays of 2019, Sabrina finished up working next door and decided to dedicate the entire summer to spending quality time with her family. Little did she know that that summer would be the island's darkest, and that within weeks her family's lives would be changed dramatically for the worst.

On 20 December 2019, several fires, sparked by lightning strikes, broke out on the north coast of Kangaroo Island. After eleven days, local firefighters and volunteers were finally able to bring them under control. However, conditions deteriorated rapidly when further lightning strikes caused several more fires that burned through inaccessible bushland and were then fuelled by strong northerly winds: it was the perfect storm. By 2 January 2020, evacuations began, and it soon became clear that lives were at stake.

Sabrina's husband had been helping fight the blazes as one of the many local farm firefighting units. In the early weeks, Sabrina's farm and home weren't directly in the path of fire and so while Ben was out defending other people's properties, Sabrina and the kids were at home managing the farm.

Each morning, they would venture out in the ute to check the boundaries, see how close the smoke was getting and ensure there were no grassfires burning. They fed their sheep and kept an ear on the radio for any emergency warnings in their area. Sabrina didn't see Ben for those first two weeks when seventeen fires burned across the region and locals needed all the support they could get.

'The only reason I knew that my husband had been home was because I found a pile of dirty laundry somewhere on the floor or an empty plate in the sink. So, I knew he had been there at some point in the night, probably for an hour, to change and go out again.'

As each day passed, Sabrina would look to the sky to see the island engulfed with more and more smoke; the fires were getting dangerously close. On 3 January 2020, winds pushed the fire directly towards their farm and eventually Sabrina and her children had no choice but to evacuate. They got out just four hours before the fire was at their front gate. While they headed to Ben's father's house in town to meet his wife, Ben insisted on staying behind, accompanied by his dad and brother, to defend the farm. Sabrina and Ben's home had been in the Davis family for three generations and they were desperate to save it. But it was no use; the inferno was unstoppable. The entire property was swallowed by flames. Ben, his father and his brother had no choice but to seek shelter in the house while the fire took everything in its path. At first, they thought the house had survived, but then they realised the fire had managed to get into the roof space. With no water or equipment left in the wake of the fire front, they were unable to do anything except helplessly watch the old farmhouse burn to the ground before they evacuated themselves along a safe route towards their families.

Meanwhile, a few hours before, Sabrina and her kids had arrived at her mother-in-law's house some 100 kilometres away from the heart of the disaster. Even while she waited for news, Sabrina never imagined what was about to happen. She remained optimistic that their farm and home would remain intact and that Ben would soon call with some uplifting news. However, as the hours passed with no communication from him and phone services down across the region, Sabrina became more and more panicked, wondering if Ben had made it out alive. Then finally, at 8 pm, hours after evacuating and with some services back online, Sabrina's phone rang.

'It was Ben. He said, "I'm okay, but I'm sorry, I couldn't save it. We lost the house. It's gone. All of it."'

Knowing her husband had survived the fire and escaped just in time was the greatest gift for Sabrina and her family. However, she then faced a new reality: they were homeless and she would have to tell the kids in the morning. Their farm had been completely incinerated; their house, sheds and machinery wiped out. More than 500 sheep, their entire farming business, had perished in the blaze, and they had nothing but the clothes on their backs and the emergency box she'd packed that now seemed absolutely insignificant.

I'm okay, but I'm sorry. I couldn't save it. We lost the house. It's gone. All of it.

'I soon realised all those official things I packed, like our passports, are actually so replaceable. What I miss the most are memories tied to the children when they were little. Scrapbooks, paintings, letters, precious things that no one can reprint for me, no one can get those back.'

The Black Summer fires of 2019–2020 were the largest in the community's recorded history and burned almost half of the island, destroying 210,000 hectares—including one of South Australia's most important ecological sites, Flinders Chase National Park. Two people were killed during the fires, along with nearly 60,000 sheep and an estimated 25,000 koalas, plus countless other habitat and wildlife. Eighty-seven homes were destroyed in the blazes; Sabrina's was one of them. When Jordan and Kerily woke up in the morning, their parents told them the devastating news, but, much to her surprise, they didn't seem to care at all about what they'd lost. Instead, they were just grateful their mum and dad were okay.

'My daughter said, "Home is where you are, Mum." And that taught me a really big lesson, because they don't care about the materialistic things like you'd think kids do. They knew all of that could be rebuilt.'

The rebuilding part of their journey has taken years, and much of the island is still recovering more than two years later. It took a full week before Sabrina mustered up the courage to return to the farm to survey the damage after the fires. By then, Ben had disposed of most of the carcasses of the animals that had perished. He tried to shield her from that trauma but it was inevitable. Sabrina cried as she drove up their one-kilometre-long driveway. In the place where her house used to stand, there was nothing but tin and rubble. Seeing their home reduced to black dust was one thing, but it was the items belonging to her children that moved her to tears: their charred bikes, their burned trampoline and the wireframe of her children's mattresses are images that are ingrained in Sabrina's mind forever.

'It was like a war zone. Everything was reduced to dust, and I just couldn't imagine how we could move on from this.'

In the aftermath of the disaster, Sabrina, Jordan and Kerily moved into a small, one-bedroom granny flat inside a shed on her father-in-law's property and stayed there for one year. Ben, on the other hand, returned to the farm the morning after the fire to start the rebuilding process, and he refused to live elsewhere, even though there were no dwellings or shelter left.

Their sheep-farming livelihood was gone and they knew they had to pick up the pieces and start again as quickly as possible. Ben spent most of that first year away from his family, initially living in a swag in the blackened bush of their property, working long days, re-fencing their farm in preparation to restock it with sheep. His uncle gave him a caravan that he lived in for six months before a donated shipping container became his new home. Ben did what most farmers do during tough times—he rolled up his sleeves and got to work.

Like so many of the families impacted, Sabrina's family relied heavily on the generosity of the community, who rallied around them and donated bags full of clothes and toiletries and delivered home-cooked meals to help get them back on their feet. They survived with whatever they were given, and Sabrina calls that her 'zombie' period, a traumatic time in her life that she only vaguely remembers because it was such an unfathomable blur of loss and grief. And at the core of it all, during her darkest days following the fires, Sabrina had to remember that she had two children she had to be strong for, even though all she wanted to do was fall apart.

'Being homeless was a pretty hard pill for me to swallow and I struggled mentally for a long time. I was a zombie for the first two months and just functioned for the children.'

Sabrina has always worked incredibly hard and gets a kick out of being productive but she admits that she felt helpless at the time when her family tried to pick up the pieces, especially knowing that her husband was out on their property every day on his own trying to rebuild everything they'd lost. Eventually, Sabrina found great purpose in focusing her efforts on the enormous pile of paperwork involved in reclaiming their lives. From insurance to grant applications to accessing funding to help replace farming machinery, Sabrina threw herself into work and found the money to make things happen and support Ben on the ground. While Sabrina and the kids visited him whenever they could, he was on the farm 100 kilometres away and logistically that was hard, so they spent most of those first twelve months apart.

> I was a zombie for the first two months and just functioned for the children.

A year later, it was clear that being apart for so long was taking its toll on them all mentally. Ben especially was struggling to live an isolated life on the farm on his own and Sabrina knew that he needed more support. So, on the first anniversary of the fire that destroyed their home, the four of them moved into temporary emergency accommodation—a small, portable shipping container with bunk beds that was delivered to their farm by the Minderoo Foundation. It was a very tight squeeze but they were so grateful! They had access to basic amenities such as a toilet,

Karen Brock in her plant laboratory, improving crop yields and resistance to disease. *Photograph: Ness Vanderburgh*

Julie McDonald and the stunning vista of her backyard. *Photograph: Eddie Safarik*

Darrylin Gordon out and about managing Lamboo Station.

Pat Fennell, with a heart still the size of Phar Lap's. *Photograph: Ali B Photography*

Danyelle Haigh trekking to the next job with her customised Mack truck.

Catriona Rowntree, *Getaway* presenter and passionate advocate of wool. *Photograph: James D. Morgan/Getty Images*

Julie Mayne, kicking back in her workshop–studio. *Photograph: Edwina Robertson*

Keelen Mailman stands her ground on Country at Mount Tabor. *Photograph: Carbon Creative*

Sabrina Davis with her two children Jordan and Kerily in the winter months following the Black Summer bushfires on Kangaroo Island.

Raine Holcombe in her element, out mustering. *Photograph: Landline*

Grace Brennan down at the stockyards with her kids Eliza (foreground), Maggie (lower fence) and Charlie (stroller).

Fleur McDonald takes a well-deserved writing break. *Photograph: Rosie Henderson*

Lyn Kelson, regenerative farmer, with Olive, her house cow.

Diana Butler enjoying time with young friends in Tanzania. *Photograph: Hayley Atkins*

Stephanie Trethewey at home on the farm recording a podcast.
*Photograph: Sophie Murfitt*

a shower, a small kitchenette and a water tank, but, most importantly, they were back together.

Sabrina and I caught up again in March 2022, more than two years after the fire. At the time, her two children were still living in the portable pod, but Sabrina and Ben needed more space after two years living on top of each other. So, they built themselves a small, 20-square-metre room next to the children which gave everyone some more freedom and room to breathe while they all eagerly watched on as their new home was built just 30 metres away from their temporary living quarters. Excitingly, just weeks after we caught up, Sabrina, Ben, Jordan and Kerily finally moved into their new home which stands proudly overlooking their farm, a testament to everything they've overcome and everything they've managed to reclaim. Seven hundred sheep now roam their property again and their business is slowly coming back to life.

'I am so excited to have a proper kitchen with an oven. I've had to get very creative with our barbecue over the past couple of years! But the most special part is all of us being under the same roof again, in our own home, sitting around a dining-room table, having friends and family come and visit.'

During the toughest years of her life, Sabrina still managed to help her community in the most extraordinary of ways.

In the wake of the fires, she founded the Humans of Kangaroo Island project which aimed to celebrate the people in her community as well as raise money to help supply farmers with personal protective equipment (PPE) equipment kits to prepare them for future fires. After Ben lost all his farm firefighting equipment and Sabrina realised they'd have to pay to replace the equipment themselves, she stepped in to help others. She started by interviewing the island's residents and posted stories alongside their portraits across her social media channels as a way to get to know her community better and raise awareness. She then leveraged its popularity by publishing a book featuring their profiles and held a fundraising event and an auction. By the end of 2021, she'd raised more than $75,000, which has gone towards providing 225 PPE kits, six strategically placed quick-fill pumps, hundreds of first aid kits and woollen blankets as well as a number of UHF radios to farmers on the island—and raising a memorial plaque to commemorate the two lives that were lost. Sabrina continues to raise money through Humans of Kangaroo Island, with additional funds now being earmarked for other causes, including rebuilding a playground at one of the island's fire-ravaged sports centres. For her incredible commitment to helping her community, Sabrina was inducted into South Australia's Women Honour Roll in 2021 and she continues to be a fierce advocate for her island home.

'The farmers now all have these kits in their utes ready to go for future fires. But when I handed them out I said, "I hope you never have to use this again."'

Not long ago, Sabrina had nothing, but from all the heartbreak she says she's gained everything. She's gained a new perspective, a new appreciation of life and a new understanding of what truly matters. So now, when she thinks about that emergency box she packed on the day she and the kids evacuated the farm, she has some words of wisdom for others. In case of an emergency, think long and hard about what you really need and what you'll really miss. Perhaps it's not the inconvenience of replacing passports and paperwork that will have the biggest impact in the wake of heartache or loss, but the imprint of those tiny hands, those paintings in scrapbooks, those cards, those love letters or the photos that captured precious moments in time.

'Time is everything; it's all we've got and no day is promised. Now that we're rebuilding the house, it's not the house itself that matters, it's what it stands for. The safety, and the security, with the people I love.'

# 10

# Raine Holcombe: The long road

## Timber Creek, Northern Territory

Raine Holcombe's teenage years and her favourite co-curricular activities were just a little different to mine. While I enjoyed swinging a tennis racquet in the city after school, Raine was swinging by a rope from a helicopter into a crocodile nest. Yep, I didn't see that coming when I first heard her story either.

Raine Holcombe is a tough-as-nails contract musterer who was raised on a crocodile farm in the Northern Territory. But while she could endure some of the toughest times on the land, wrangling crocs and living in isolation, she never imagined that her dream of wrangling her own children would prove to be the toughest challenge of her life. Surviving swimming in crocodile-infested waters seems like a piece of cake in comparison.

'For years, I couldn't bring myself to even sit with the women at social events and listen to them talk about their children, it was just too painful. I'd go off and talk to the blokes.'

An only child, Raine was born in Katherine and grew up on a property in the Victoria River region. Her parents had crocs, not cows, and owned a thriving business with up to 7000 crocodiles on their station at any one time. They managed the entire process from incubating and hatching eggs through to growing out crocs until they were a couple of metres in length. The animals would be processed for meat and sold domestically and internationally, their sought-after skins sent to Italy, Japan and France. Sourcing and raising this luxury niche product is not for the faint-hearted, and the whole process is very labour intensive, especially the initial wild egg hunt, which brings us back to Raine swinging off a rope, suspended from a helicopter.

Each year, the team would head out camping for a couple of days in the bush to collect crocodile eggs and transport them to an incubator on the farm. On average, they would achieve an 80–85 per cent survival rate for the eggs and hatchlings, whereas in the wild, because of predators, it's as little as 1 per cent. As a child, Raine begged to go out with her dad and their chopper pilot for the annual egg hunt and finally, at sixteen, she was given the green light to join them. She was thrilled to be hanging precariously off the helicopter, collecting croc nests and hoping that a very angry mother croc wasn't lurking nearby, ready to pounce.

Raine never got into any trouble on these trips, but her father once had a very lucky escape. Raine watched, horrified, as he was winched empty-handed back to the chopper with holes all through his shirt. A mother croc had lunged up from underneath her nest and pinned him down, her jaw clenched across his chest and back. They quickly flew him to the nearest First Nations community and there he was stitched up and sent home with quite the tale to tell, although he wasn't game enough to tell Raine's mother what had happened.

'I don't know if the helicopter scared the mother croc away but she spat him out. And we're very grateful because if she'd got him in the water, we would never have seen him again.'

Raine's closest call with a croc wasn't in the wild but at home on the farm. When she was nine years old she went for a swim in a pond that her mum and dad had dug near their house in preparation for a future swimming pool. In the wet season, rain would fill the hole, turning it into a muddy, makeshift pool, and, as it was a particularly hot day, Raine and one of her parents' employees hopped in for a quick dip to cool off. But then things took a terrifying turn. After a few moments, Raine felt something sharp brush up against her leg and foot. At first, she thought perhaps it was the worker playing a joke on her underwater—well, it wasn't. Within seconds, Raine saw the worker on the other side of the pool as the unmistakable clamp of a crocodile's jaws gripped her leg. It started to thrash around, attempting what's known as a 'death roll', a spinning manoeuvre used by crocodiles to subdue prey underwater. Then, incredibly, the young croc released Raine's leg for just a moment, and she was able to hastily climb out of the pond, crying and screaming for her parents. The croc was only a metre in length but could easily have killed a nine-year-old Raine if it had pulled her underwater for long enough. Thankfully she escaped with just a few stitches, a scar, one hell of a dinner party story and one special keepsake she still has today.

'After it happened, my dad ran to get an outdoor chair and sat beside the pond with a stubby and his rifle, waiting for the crocodile to surface. When it did, he shot it and I still have the skin on my floor.'

It's safe to say that Raine had a very unconventional childhood on the station and she loved every minute of it. She completed her primary school education remotely via School of the Air, taught by her mother, before heading off to boarding school in Rockhampton for Year 8. This was a big move for Raine, and she found the transition very hard to begin with as she'd never been away from her parents before, let alone sat in a real classroom with other kids. After a difficult first year, she finally found her feet and made some lifelong friends.

In Year 10 she started studying for her pilot's licence, planning to head back to the land and find a job mustering cattle from the air. After graduating high school, she returned to her parents' property to work and started saving the money she needed to complete her pilot studies. However, she soon realised that she enjoyed being on the ground more than being in the air and she was eager to get some station experience mustering by horseback. Two years later, at twenty years of age, she left home for a whole new adventure.

In 2008, Raine started working as a first-year jillaroo out on Bunda Station, six hours from Katherine, learning the ropes of cattle station life and dating one of the workers whose family owned a contract mustering business near Fitzroy Crossing in Western Australia. Their relationship progressed, and when he was invited home to help manage his family's business he asked Raine to join him. In 2009, the couple made the move west and Raine was thrust headfirst into the mustering world, moving mobs of thousands of cattle in the outback and living her jillaroo dream. But only a year after moving there, Raine and her boyfriend separated and her time on the station came to a bit of an awkward end. Raine found another job working on Coolibah Station, back in the Northern Territory, before moving on again to a bigger role that would ultimately change her life.

In 2011, Raine moved to Kidman's Springs Research Station in the Victoria River region, a 32,000-hectare property owned by the government for research purposes. It was here one weekend that she reconnected with her future husband at a local campdraft where they were both competing. Raine had briefly met Tristram, affectionately known as 'Potter', during her time at Bunda Station a few years earlier and they had become friends. After meeting at the campdraft and bonding over their shared love for horses, the two of them quickly became much more than mates.

'It all really started between us after he invited himself to my parents' croc farm for a weekend. He asked to join me and that was that. His pestering paid off!'

Potter ran his own contract mustering business, and after dating for a few months Raine decided to take the plunge and join him in the business as his right-hand woman. She's been by his side ever since. In the early years, when Raine went out to the stock camps with Potter, they lived in a gooseneck trailer for most of the year, travelling from station to station for mustering jobs from February to November and returning home to Raine's parents' place for a break in the wet season. Despite their isolation on the road, without internet or phone service, Raine calls their gooseneck set-up 'glamping', aka glamorous camping.

'We're lucky to be mustering in the modern era. They definitely did it tough back in the day, living in swags with a fire.

We've got a shipping container decked out as a kitchen and a few other mod cons!'

After working together for a couple of years and realising they 'weren't going to kill each other' in the process, Potter got down on one knee in one of the paddocks on her parents' farm and proposed to Raine, surrounded by her favourite horses. Twelve months later, they tied the knot on the same property. Family and friends travelled across the country, packing their swags and bringing their campervans to celebrate at the place where Raine had grown up. And, as is the case for so many newlyweds, the moment the big day is over you're flooded with questions about when you plan to start a family. For Raine and Potter, these questions proved to be more and more painful as the months and years went on. Raine had always dreamed of having children, but after twelve months of trying to conceive naturally, they realised that they were going to need some help. Living remotely made the quest to access medical services and expertise extremely difficult, and unfortunately this was a situation they had to endure for several more years.

In November 2017, Raine and Potter started their first round of IVF and were referred to a clinic in Darwin. It was their closest option and a seven-hour drive from the property where they were stationed as part of their mustering contract. The first stage of the IVF process included countless appointments, scans, medications and then finally egg-retrieval surgery, which meant that Raine needed to book accommodation in Darwin for three weeks. Her mum joined her so she wasn't alone—Potter had to keep the wheels turning and couldn't leave their mustering contract. From that initial egg retrieval, Raine and Potter were able to get six frozen embryos, which they were told was promising. From there, Raine had to prepare herself for her first embryo transfer, and during one particular week she had to have a blood test every couple of days as part of the preparation. This meant she had to travel a four-hour round trip from the station to a tiny town of Tennant Creek to have those tests done before they were sent to Darwin.

'Often our results would get lost, or they didn't make it to Darwin in time, or you'd have to go back and get the test done again. And I guess that's part of the downside of living rural, and remote medical facilities and access are not as reliable as they are in the city.'

Heartbreakingly, twelve months and three failed rounds of IVF later, Raine and Potter were no closer to having the baby they desperately wanted. None of the tests offered to them at the time provided any real answers as to why they weren't able to conceive. It's at that point that they lost confidence in their IVF clinic in Darwin and sought some advice from interstate specialists who could provide them with a fresh perspective and new options. They found a highly regarded IVF specialist on the Gold Coast who said he was disappointed with their previous clinic and the limited testing they did. This gave Raine a glimmer of hope that they would soon find a solution.

Raine went in for another round of egg-collection surgery in 2018, this time travelling thousands of kilometres to the Gold Coast and staying for the same three-week process she'd been through before. Twice the number of eggs were retrieved this time and another nine embryos were created, which meant Raine and Potter had twelve embryos on ice. Their Gold Coast specialist immediately ordered a pre-implantation screening test on the embryos to ensure there were no genetic abnormalities.

> Often our results would get lost, or they didn't make it to Darwin in time, or you'd have to go back and get the test done again.

After those results came back clear, Raine went in for another embryo transfer but sadly that too failed. Over the following six months, she underwent a further two rounds of IVF, both of which were unsuccessful. At that point, almost three years into their fertility journey, Raine and Potter weren't sure how much more they could endure. The phone calls from medical staff with the same words—'I'm sorry'—were becoming too much to bear; the daily medications hormonal injections were taking their toll physically and emotionally.

'It was soul-crushing. I couldn't put a price on a family and the ultimate goal in my life was to have children, but at that point we'd spent over $100,000 on IVF. The financial strain was huge. We had to re-evaluate everything.'

Thankfully, Raine and Potter had a doctor who simply would not give up. After each failed round of IVF, he had tried something new—a new medication or another blood test—to investigate other possible causes of their fertility struggles. After six failed embryo transfers and immeasurable heartache, he suggested there was still one possible reason Raine and Potter couldn't conceive, and all it took to find out was one relatively inexpensive blood test. No one else had proposed this in the three years prior. Raine and Potter were tested for what is known as the DQ alpha gene. The DQ alpha gene sits within our immune system and one of its key roles is to help the body identify, fight and prevent foreign antigens from making us sick. If the couple trying to conceive have an exact genetic match for the DQa and share the same gene profile for that chromosome, this disrupts the connection between the sperm and the uterus. Instead of signalling to the uterus that the sperm is okay to implant, the uterus attacks the sperm, viewing it as a risk, and therefore eliminates the embryo. That blood test came back and concluded that Raine and Potter were a complete match.

'We couldn't believe that all that time all we needed was one blood test to uncover the issue. It was bittersweet, but also a huge blow because we were then told we only had a 20 per cent chance of ever conceiving a child.'

Raine and Potter's options were to either use a surrogate to carry one of their embryos, use donor sperm to create embryos Raine's body wouldn't attack or try a revolutionary treatment called lymphocyte immunisation therapy (LIT). They opted for LIT, which involved travelling to Melbourne twice in two months. Doctors isolated white blood cells from Potter and injected them into Raine with the aim of acclimatising her body to the foreign cells and eventually accepting an embryo. In January 2020, three-and-a-half years after first trying for a baby and after undergoing LIT treatment, Raine had another single embryo transfer but heartbreakingly that round also failed. Raine had suffered from endometriosis, so she underwent a laparoscopy to remove any remaining cysts and scar tissue in a last-ditch attempt to prepare her body for final IVF round. A month later, on 27 February 2020, a rather downcast Raine went in for her eighth embryo transfer, and this time two embryos were implanted to give her the best chance of success. Incredibly, just a couple of weeks later, Raine and Potter got the phone call they'd been dreaming of for almost four years. They were finally pregnant.

'You get the phone call from the nurse and you just expect the worst news again. This time it was just so unbelievable because we'd never been that close, we'd never achieved a pregnancy. There were so many mixed emotions.'

Their excitement was short-lived and was followed by complete panic and anxiety. The week after discovering they were pregnant, week seven, Raine started bleeding heavily. She rushed to hospital for a scan that revealed that she had in fact been pregnant with twins (which she didn't know) but had lost one. Thankfully, one strong heartbeat remained and Raine tentatively embraced the remainder of the pregnancy, feeling incredibly apprehensive for the first two trimesters, terrified she would lose this baby too. She remained on a strict immune protocol with regular injections and tablets to help suppress her immune system further to keep the pregnancy viable. At this point, life in the stock camp took a very different turn for Raine. She was used to working alongside Potter, mustering cattle on horseback and getting her hands dirty with all the jobs that had to be done, but he had grown increasingly cautious about allowing Raine to do anything physical, worried about the health of the baby. It was a challenging and frustrating time for Raine as she tried to take it easy but she knew it would all be worth it. And as her baby continued to grow inside her, she slowly allowed herself to feel excited and hopeful that her dream of motherhood was finally becoming a reality.

On 10 November 2020, Raine arrived at Katherine Hospital for a planned C-section as her baby was breech. As she was wheeled into theatre she felt calm and ready. The bright lights of the surgery didn't phase her at all as she'd already been through so much with so many procedures over the past few years. When it was finally time to meet their baby, the moment felt incredibly surreal for Raine and Potter. Minutes later, doctors lifted up a healthy little girl who came out screaming—music to their ears! Their miracle baby was finally here after a heart-wrenching journey that had lasted four-and-a-half years. It almost felt too good to be true.

'I started breastfeeding straight away and sat in recovery for a few hours. It was a really special time, to get to the point where we were finally able to hold our very healthy baby. It was surreal and I don't think the reality of it hit me for a couple of weeks.'

Raine and Potter named their little girl Hallie. After leaving hospital a few days later, they brought her home to the small block of land they'd purchased the year before in the tiny rural town of Timber Creek on the banks of the Victoria River, and over the next couple weeks they settled into their new life as parents. They were exceptionally grateful that Raine's roller-coaster pregnancy was in fact perfectly timed, with Hallie arriving at the end of the mustering season, just in time for the wet. This meant Potter was able to be home with his girls for the first couple of months, before heading back out to contract muster on a station two hours away. He left when Hallie was three months old but Raine had prepared for this and was determined to stay close as a family and bring Hallie along for the ride when she could. So a few weeks later, Raine and Hallie ventured off to join Potter and the mustering crew and would continue to make the long journey out to the stock camp every week for a night or two so they could all be together.

The gooseneck in which Raine and Potter had spent their pre-parenthood days certainly needed a few updates to ensure it was equipped for a baby on board. Several cupboards were emptied to make way for Hallie's items, a porta-cot with a clip-on change table was squeezed into a corner and, crucially, they invested in voice-activated, handheld radios, which allowed Hallie to sleep soundly in the air-conditioned gooseneck during the steaming hot summer days and nights and Raine could hear her when she woke up.

'She's adapted so well, and she loves being bathed in the sink down in the camp area. She brings a bit of joy to the crew too.'

For most of their mustering adventures together, Raine and Hallie travel at the back of the mob with Hallie strapped into a baby seat in the ute. Listening to Raine describe an average day, you'd have to say Hallie is the most patient baby in the world, sitting in the vehicle for hours at a time, happily gazing out of the window, demolishing snacks and watching hundreds, sometimes thousands, of head of cattle being mustered.

Occasionally, Raine would ask the stock camp cook to jump in the ute with Hallie and take over the driving, so Raine could get back in the saddle and ride ahead with the crew, doing what she loves.

'In the first few months, if something was wrong or Hallie needed me, the cook would just call me on the radio and I'd ride my horse back to the car and breastfeed Hallie or whatever she needed, and then once she was happy again, I'd jump back on my horse.'

> She's adapted so well, and she loves being bathed in the sink down in the camp area.

Life on the road with Hallie has been full of adventure, and Raine has thrived throughout motherhood, regularly sharing her life with her online community via social media. And as Hallie has grown from newborn to toddler, Raine has shared her dreams of giving her a sibling. In November 2021 when Hallie was a year old, Raine and Potter began the IVF process once again, with Raine travelling to the Gold Coast for weeks of treatment to prepare her body for another egg collection. Three new embryos were created, genetically tested and then frozen, with a plan to begin the transfer process in March 2022. However, a few days after her egg-retrieval surgery, Raine noticed that her period was late which was baffling but intriguing. Always the optimist, she took a home pregnancy test. To her complete shock, two lines appeared—she was pregnant. Raine and Potter conceived naturally for the first time, which went against all medical opinions including her specialist, who told Raine that with her and Potter's DQ alpha gene match Raine's immune system would become more aggressive with each pregnancy, making conception even harder than it had been in the past.

'We couldn't believe it. You hear about these stories, but I never imagined it would be us. Potter was like, oh my God, we just spent $15,000 on this latest IVF round and now we've fallen pregnant naturally!'

Raine is a couple of months pregnant when we catch up to discuss the book, and things have been going well. Looking back on the past six years fills Raine with overwhelming gratitude but also a hint of frustration at the rural healthcare system that let her down. Four years of heartache trying to start a family that could very well have been avoided or significantly reduced if a simple blood test had been offered to them early on. She now dedicates much of her time sharing her journey to her many rural followers, shining a light on infertility in the bush. She calls herself the 'IVF Cowgirl' under the Instagram handle 'barren_old_cow'.

We just spent $15,000 on this latest IVF round and now we've fallen pregnant naturally!

'There needs to be more attention given to rural families and fertility. Everyone deserves the same chance at a family, no matter where you live, and early intervention and testing need to be more available. It's as simple as that.'

Raine tentatively but excitedly navigated her way through this pregnancy, preparing to pack another porta-cot and give glamping life another red-hot crack, and on 19 September 2022 she gave birth to Stirling Edward Owen Holcombe, her second miracle.

'I'm not sure where we're going to fit two kids in the gooseneck though, but we'll find a way. I think we're going to have to put an air conditioner in the horse section and convert that into another room!'

# 11

# Grace Brennan: The drought that changed everything

## Warren, New South Wales

In October 2019, Grace Brennan sat at her kitchen table on her farm and started a social media account that very quickly and unexpectedly changed her life and the lives of thousands of others across rural Australia. At the time, she was upset and frustrated, having witnessed the devastating impact of crippling drought on her local community in north-west New South Wales, as well as what was happening to other farmers and their families around the country.

'People were going out of business, people were depressed, people were suffering, and there seemed to be a lot of talk around relief funding but not a lot of immediate action.'

So Grace took action. Through a simple, innovative idea that connects bush businesses to city audiences, she helped put drought on the national stage and saved many struggling outback businesses from ruin.

While Grace is now an adored face of rural Australia, she grew up a very long way from any cows or crops. The youngest of five kids, she was raised in Sydney's Lane Cove and enjoyed a blissful suburban childhood. She was very into sport, netball in particular, competing in the first division State League and playing indoor netball for New South Wales. Her rock-solid reflexes and strong hand-eye coordination came in very handy on Halloween in 1997, the night that ultimately marked the beginning of the rest of her life. Grace was fourteen years old and enjoying a sleepover at her friend's house. The group of girls she was with wanted to go out trick-or-treating but Grace wasn't really that interested. She was too busy watching *Outback Adventures with Troy Dann*, a TV show that took viewers to the most remote corners of outback Australia, sharing its history and wildlife. Grace had never set foot on a station but she was hooked.

'It was a dose of the outback on the screen and it was a whole new and foreign world. I was fascinated!'

Eventually, Grace's friends persuaded her to venture out for a bit of Halloween mischief, so off they all went, down the street. Suddenly, out of the blue, several dark-hooded figures emerged and the girls realised they were under egg attack from a group of teenage boys.

'One of them threw an egg at me. I caught it and threw it back and got him! His name was Jack.'

Jack was a country boy boarding at the high school just across the road from the house where Grace was staying. When one of her friends made fun of her in front of the boys they'd just met, revealing that she would have preferred to stay home and watch a TV show on outback Australia, Jack swooped to her defence. And that, as she describes it, was the beginning of her lifelong crush. Over the next couple of years, their teenage relationship blossomed and it became very clear to everyone that the pair was inseparable. This was more than just a high school fling.

To Grace, Jack was an entirely different species of male teenager. You couldn't mistake him for anything other than a country boy. For a start, he dressed differently from the city schoolboys. He wore boots, Wrangler jeans and a shirt with his collar flipped up. He was confident but a gentleman and he looked Grace straight in the eye whenever she was talking—which was, at times, unnerving. Jack related to adults in a way that Grace felt could only come from working on a farm where he was treated as an adult, working alongside his dad who was both his colleague and his boss. Jack wasn't afraid to face the hard stuff either, and Grace was instantly attracted to his maturity and the way carried himself.

'You know in those teenage years when the shit hits the fan at some sort of occasion and everybody just cowers thinking, oh, my God, shit, we can't tell the parents. Well, Jack would just stand up and walk towards them and face it head on. That was really appealing to me.'

The land was in Jack's blood, and as their relationship grew more serious Grace was invited out to his family's farm for her first taste of country life. She was sixteen when she first ventured out to their property at Warren, six hours from Sydney. Grace felt like she was getting to know a whole new side of Jack, and it became clear just how much of a fish out of water he was in the city and how much of a fish out of water she was in his world. Her trips to the farm during their teenage years felt like a holiday at times, with Jack taking Grace out yabbying and fishing, preparing her meals and showing her the ropes. On occasion, Grace would sit back and watch Jack and his dad or uncle work in the sheep yards and sometimes she'd offer to help, although that raised a few eyebrows in the beginning.

'I remember one time when I was helping with the sheep, I asked if they had gardening gloves that I could wear so that I didn't get the burrs in my hands, which like, honestly! They would have just thought I was such a sook!'

The responsibility Jack had at age sixteen was unbelievable to Grace. It was becoming very clear that the country was calling, and at some point he would want to return home to the farm where he was raised to carry on the family legacy. But there were still adventures to be had that would take them both well outside their comfort zones. After graduating high school, Grace and Jack took a gap year and travelled around Europe and the UK before returning to Sydney where Grace began a double degree—a Bachelor of Arts in international studies that involved a year studying abroad in Chile. Jack joined her for six months and the pair immersed themselves in a whole new culture in Santiago. It was a very significant year for Grace because she knew deep down that when she returned home to Australia she'd soon be moving to the bush, so she made the most of it.

When they returned to Sydney, Jack finished his degree in agricultural economics, and before the ink was dry on his final assessment he was on his way home, back to Warren, back to the land and back to the family business. Grace decided she wasn't quite ready to give up her city life and commit to the bush just yet, so she decided to stay in Sydney for another year, working at a local council in a community development role, which she loved. She wanted to get some work experience under her belt and buy herself some time to come to terms with the idea that she was old enough and ready enough to commit to a life in rural Australia with the man she loved. Meanwhile, Jack had bought into the family farm after his uncle left the business. He was going through a truly transformational period of his life, with real skin in the game that took his role and plans to a whole new level. By 2009, Grace and Jack were ready to make the leap together, although it was Grace who had to give up everything she'd ever known, including the familiarity of the city, the proximity of her family and friends and a career she'd only just begun. It wasn't easy at first.

'When it was time to actually cut the cord and make the move, I realised that even though conceptually I probably knew that it was always in my future, I don't think I really knew what I was in for.'

Grace was 25 years old when she packed her Toyota Corolla (the most impractical little car for the bush) to the brim and prepared to make the six-hour journey from Sydney to the outskirts of Warren. Jack of course was there for the big day, helping with the move (and squeezing the rest of her stuff into his ute). Grace said a teary goodbye to her family, and she and Jack travelled in convoy across New South Wales towards their future together. Grace admits now that the tears flooded out of her the entire drive.

'It was just this feeling that you've fallen in love with a farmer, and you're moving to the land and, basically, it's forever. Farming life is not some passing phase that they're going to go through and come out of. And the gravity of my decision was dawning on me, that feeling of forever and the fact that you've got to love this life, no matter what.'

Grace and Jack moved into the original homestead his dad had grown up in, which was surrounded by 4000 hectares of dry-land cropping and sheep country. The house hadn't been lived in for many years and needed some TLC, so Grace got to work, stripping up carpet and hanging curtains in her bid to set down roots and make the place their own. It was a difficult time for her. She'd left home but didn't quite feel at home in her new environment. And she had moved up at the very busiest time for Jack—harvest. The stark reality of his working life confronted her head on.

'The very first morning I woke up in this little cottage in the middle of nowhere, all alone. Jack had headed off to work on the farm at 5 am and I just thought, what the hell am I going to do?'

> The gravity of my decision was dawning on me, that feeling of forever and the fact that you've got to love this life, no matter what.

Grace found her feet in the community pretty quickly, though. She threw herself into work opportunities, spending her first twelve months working for the state government managing an Indigenous youth engagement project, then moving into an executive role at the Far West Academy of Sport. In the meantime, just a few months after Grace made the big country move, Jack proposed at a romantic picnic of prawns and champagne, set up in a paddock. They tied the knot on the family farm in 2010, after an incredible growing season that produced their biggest wheat crop in years. There was much to celebrate, especially because the newlyweds had bought into the family business, taking on a significant debt in the process, so the bumper season was just what they needed. But Grace was about to witness firsthand just how unpredictable Mother Nature is and how quickly she can turn.

When Grace and Jack returned from their honeymoon in time for harvest, it started raining. Not the good kind of rain craved by farmers battling drought but the bad kind. Too much and too quickly. The rain was relentless and, within weeks, Grace and Jack's crops were completely flooded and ruined. It was a devastating financial blow for the young couple just finding their feet in the business and quite a frightening time, with flood levels rising so high that water lapped at their front door. For several weeks they were cut off from the local town of Warren and the only way to get groceries and supplies was to have them flown into the farm by helicopter.

'I'll never forget that knot in my stomach and my throat, listening to endless rain on a tin roof and knowing what it was doing.'

The honeymoon was well and truly over, and Grace was very quickly getting a taste for the harsh reality that many farmers face. Their first season together was incredibly tough but they picked themselves up, optimistic about the next year's harvest. Then, at the same time during harvest the following year, the Warren region was hit with another big rain event and although this one wasn't quite as devastating for the town, it still caused significant flooding and washed out Grace and Jack's crops for the second year in a row. At the time, Grace was heavily pregnant with their first child, Eliza, and when she gave birth in December 2011 the farm was in the middle of a harvest frenzy. Jack and the farm workers were trying to salvage whatever crops they could. Jack was under enormous pressure to help steer the family business through a difficult time and Grace was left feeling incredibly isolated and untethered as a first-time mum, a far cry from the journey into motherhood she had hoped for or expected.

'I turned my phone on silent when Eliza was born, and I haven't really had it on the normal audible sound since. I just couldn't handle the outside invasion because there was enough going on at home and I was overwhelmed.'

While Grace was busy adjusting to motherhood and getting to know baby Eliza, there were big decisions to be made about their farm. After two years of flooding and crop losses, she and Jack decided to lease out and eventually to sell the property.

> I'll never forget that knot in my stomach and my throat, listening to endless rain on a tin roof and knowing what it was doing.

In the meantime, they'd welcomed their second baby, Maggie, and were about to welcome their third, Charlie. Life was busy and very full for Grace who did everything she could to support her children and her husband while their family unit reset their goals and realigned their expectations of life on the land.

Grace and Jack settled into the new corporate farm operation, a cropping and sheep enterprise set on a 20,000-hectare property, five times the size of their family farm. The first couple of years passed quickly. By 2017, they were both working and juggling three young children, oblivious to the fact that Mother Nature was about to deliver her next cruel blow. This time a slow burn would set off a chain of events that would ultimately redirect Grace's path, changing her life and the lives of many others.

Unlike flood disasters, drought consumes the land slowly over weeks, months and sometimes years. In 2017, the Warren region was drying up quickly and there hadn't been a drop of rain in months. Grass was running out and livestock were growing increasingly hungry. Eventually, the situation became so dire that Jack made the decision to feed the stock every day to keep them alive. This time Grace and Jack had some income security, but that didn't alleviate the day-in, day-out stress of managing a deteriorating landscape and hungry animals. The drought was relentless, with no end in sight, and by 2019 the situation was critical. Grace was shocked by the toll the strain was taking in the farming community and heartbroken for her region and its people.

'Friends and neighbours were very worried about their partners and their friends. The thought of suicide was definitely a concern.'

Energy and spirits faded further and the drought edged into its third year. Farmers lost their livelihoods, animals perished and local businesses were struggling. Grace was working for an online employment platform that connected jobseekers in agriculture with employers. Naturally, job opportunities on the land became fewer and further between as the drought raged on, so work slowed down for Grace too. While our TVs were bombarded with images of drought-stricken landscapes and politicians promising financial relief, Grace felt compelled to do something that could make an immediate impact. On 16 October 2019, she set up an Instagram account called Buy From The Bush and started showcasing the beautiful things available to buy from rural communities facing drought. It was a simple idea, but it quickly grew into a highly effective movement.

'The catalyst for creating it was listening to an interview on the radio. The drought was being discussed by the prime minister and a journalist, but the need at that time was so immediate, their talk of funding just didn't seem enough.'

Many women in drought-affected areas had taken on bigger jobs, more hours, or started side hustles and small businesses to compensate for the lack of income from the farms they lived on. Over the years, Grace had fallen in love with small businesses in country towns like hers and would take her visiting city friends and family to her favourite boutiques. Invariably, her friends loved the products but didn't love that they couldn't buy online when they got back to the city, since a lot of the small businesses didn't have an e-commerce site. Grace wanted to share the products with the masses and inject much needed money into drought-crippled regions, so Buy From The Bush evolved into an online platform and retail site for bush businesses, creating an immediate bridge to city consumers.

> The drought was being discussed . . . but the need at that time was so immediate, their talk of funding just didn't seem enough.

The call for help was heard loud and clear, and the results of Grace's Buy From the Bush campaign were extraordinary. A total of $5 million in revenue was generated for the featured businesses in just four months, and 20 per cent of businesses employed additional staff as a direct result of Buy From The Bush. Shops and businesses were out of stock and on outback stations utes were loaded up with parcels to be transported across Australia and the globe. The movement put bush businesses on the map, and while Grace was busy growing her new business baby she also found out she was unexpectedly pregnant with her fourth child—an overwhelmingly exciting but daunting piece of news.

'I think Jack was thinking, oh, my God, I'm going to be needed and I've got nothing to give, because he was on the back of a few years of drought. We were concerned how we'd cope but at the same time we were thrilled.'

Then thankfully the rain started falling and Grace and Jack welcomed their fourth child in April 2020, a little girl they named August. After three years of heartbreaking conditions, the drought finally broke just before sowing began, and the relief was immense. Downpours kickstarted new life, farmers planted their crops, desperate to leverage the opportunity, and the grass finally started to grow. The energy was high again in the town of Warren but the rest of the world was shutting down as a disaster of a different kind struck—the COVID-19 pandemic. While many people, particularly in the cities, were encountering lockdowns and restrictions, Grace and Jack, along with the rest of their community, were counting their blessings.

'All my friends in the city were all in a panic about COVID and I couldn't give two shits about it. We had so much happening on the farm!'

But not all farming businesses were able to get back on their feet immediately. It's easy to assume that once it rains and the drought breaks, there's immediate relief for farmers. But in reality it takes time for producers to work with the seasonal cycle and get back up and running. A lot of machinery had been unused for more than two years during the drought and now needed repairs, and many producers didn't have the cash flow to fix things straight away. But the rain did signal the end of a bleak chapter and, slowly, the farming community started to rebuild and get back on track.

'There was quite a disconnect between urban and rural Australia because, you know, what was important to my friends and family in the city was less important to us. It was quite an interesting time, actually. If I told my city friends that it had rained and we were going to start farming again, I don't think they would have necessarily cared much at the time.'

Grace encountered another interesting moment that could be interpreted as the mainstream media's addiction to negative news. Prior to the drought breaking, she had a TV crew do some filming with her for a story about the drought and her work with Buy From The Bush. But when the rain came and conditions eased for farmers, she got a text message from the crew to say they wouldn't continue filming the story and they'd be in touch in the future. Potentially the angle was less interesting without a crisis, and as a former journalist I know this to be true of news media. Grace is passionate about ensuring we focus on long-term impacts and sustainable strategies, not just crisis relief to support rural communities through their worst times. By the time a news crew cares, you know things are very dire; unfortunately, news crews rarely stick around for some of the toughest times—the recovery.

In 2020, Grace Brennan was given the honour of delivering the Australia Day address. She talked passionately about the need to bridge the city and country divide and her speech was broadcast to millions of households across the country. She lifted spirits and she lifted backsides off seats for a standing ovation that has inspired many.

The Buy From The Bush campaign since generated $9 million in revenue for bush businesses in its first two years and is giving hope to a new generation of country entrepreneurs. One of those entrepreneurs could very well be Grace's daughter Eliza who is ten years old and interrupts when I call Grace for a quick word.

'Sorry, Eliza's just started a jewellery business online and I told her she could create an Instagram account to sell online but only if I vet the posts first. Anyway, she's just told me that she "accidentally" hit post.'

Five minutes later on the same call, Grace is negotiating snack time and sternly telling two-year-old August not to open the bag of marshmallows she's sneakily grabbed. Like so many mums, Grace wears all the hats, all the time. Her next chapter is challenging herself to manage a flexible bush business that allows working mothers like herself to thrive and stretch themselves as businesswomen living on the land while still fully owning their role as mothers. It's a life and a juggle Grace says she never in her wildest dreams imagined for herself.

And to think it all started with an attempted egg to the face.

# 12

# Fleur McDonald: The story behind the author

## Esperance, Western Australia

What could be more intimidating for a rookie writer (that's me) than penning a chapter in my first book about one of the country's most successful authors? Oh, and then sending it to her for her approval? Not much, I'll give you the hot tip. My fingers were almost trembling when I hit 'send' on an email to Fleur McDonald with this chapter. At one point, I even contemplated asking her to ghost-write her part, perhaps the entire book for me, because then it would probably be perfect. But, while I'm no award-winning author, I know that this story, Fleur's story, is one that someone else had to write because Fleur is too humble to tell it like this.

Fleur makes a living from her imagination. She has carved out an incredible career as one of Australia's most celebrated rural authors, with her gripping fictional crime novels inspired by her life on the land. But what Fleur rarely opens up about is the non-fiction reality of her own life, her extraordinary journey as a rural mother and her unconventional road to publishing success.

'Steph, I've never talked about my life so openly with someone. And while I've been through a fair bit of crap, I regret nothing.'

Fleur McDonald grew up on the southern end of the Flinders Ranges in South Australia in the small rural town of Orroroo. She lived with her parents, her brother and her sister in a house next door to the family's truck depot, which was the centre of her father's fuel distribution business, a company that had been in the family since the 1800s. Her father went on to become a trucking pioneer, recognised for being instrumental in introducing triple road trains to the Australian outback, opening up jobs and opportunities for the delivery of goods across more than a quarter of the country. Fleur is very proud of him and has fond memories of her childhood, her connection to the outback starting when she was a young girl, spending hours on end with her dad in his truck, driving around the region making deliveries.

Fleur and her siblings attended the local primary school and had a carefree childhood running amok in town and spending a lot of time with their grandparents on her mother's side, who lived on a 6500-hectare sheep station nearby. Over the years, the land seeped into Fleur's bones and all she dreamed about was working on a farm one day, immersed in the agriculture sector. So she found it extremely difficult when it was time for her to leave home at twelve years old and head off to boarding school in Adelaide, more than three hours away from her local community.

'I absolutely hated it. I don't like rules and regulations and I've always pushed boundaries, so boarding school was a disaster for me. I felt like all my freedoms had been taken away.'

Fleur admits she was a bit of a rebel child throughout high school, regularly getting up to mischief. Throughout her later teens, she'd cheekily save up her pocket money each week and head to a local pub with some friends to buy a hip flask of brandy and scotch. There's no doubt that Fleur was a free spirit and she pushed the boundaries wherever she could. As a result, her teenage years were particularly challenging as she grappled with what she wanted versus what society expected from her. In Year 10 she was so fed up with school that she wrote her dear grandfather 'Papa' a letter, begging him for a job on his sheep station so she could leave the big smoke and kickstart her life on the land. To her surprise and excitement, he said yes! However, one minor detail he overlooked was discussing this potential move with Fleur's parents, who had no idea that Fleur was so serious about dropping out of school and who promptly shut the idea down. They expected Fleur to finish school, hoping she'd eventually go to university and achieve some kind of formal qualification. But all that these expectations did was fuel Fleur's fury and determination to do things her way.

'I just decided, well, I'm going to buck the system and I'm going to work on the land, whether they like it or not.'

Fleur didn't try very hard in the classroom for the remainder of high school and didn't care much for her grades. However, no matter how little she studied, she was undeniably naturally talented in the subject of English. To her astonishment, she scored 100 per cent in her Year 12 English exam. Little did she know that her natural flair for writing would one day be her saving grace.

> I just decided, well, I'm going to buck the system and I'm going to work on the land.

Fleur was reluctant to attend high school but once she came to the end of her final year, she decided to apply to Marcus Oldham College, which is based in Victoria and is Australia's only independent higher education agricultural institution. To gain entry to their farm management program, Fleur needed two years of hands-on work experience in farming, so she applied for some jillaroo jobs and snapped up her first gig on a station at Meningie on the south-east coast of South Australia. She was one of the first female jillaroos in that area of South Australia, and she went head-to-head with the blokes for twelve months, learning the ropes and perfecting her farming skills, doing everything from shearing sheep and moving cattle to fencing and pulling newborn calves. For her second year jillarooing in 1993, Fleur moved to a station in Western Australia, some eight hours' drive from Perth. It was unlike anything Fleur had seen before.

'Coming from the Flinders Ranges, we don't get a lot of rain up there: it gets so dry. But here I was sloshing through clover plants that were 15 centimetres high and the water was up to my ankles in some of the puddles. I just didn't know that there was land like this around.'

On one of those wet days, Fleur was stomping through a tiger snake–infested swamp of reeds, tasked with the rather unglamorous job of destroying rabbit warrens as wild rabbits are a widespread and destructive agricultural pest.

A young man whom we'll call Neil (not his real name) was working in a nearby paddock, harvesting clover, and he saw her scouring the swampland. He approached her and they got chatting. This chance meeting was a sliding-door moment for Fleur. What started as a few catch-ups and casual drinks at the pub soon turned into much more. Neil was a young, ambitious farmer who had bought some of his own cattle, was leasing some land nearby and had big plans to buy his own farm one day and set up a bigger operation. Fleur was incredibly excited at the prospect of building a life on the land with him and starting a family—two things she'd always dreamed of doing.

After Fleur finished her second year of jillarooing in Western Australia, she moved to Victoria to complete her undergraduate degree at college, managing a long-distance relationship with Neil for a year. They were happy enough as a couple, but even in these early stages of their relationship there were difficulties that Fleur didn't pay too much attention at the time. Since leaving school and being accepted into university, she'd had her heart set on studying farm management, but Neil told her that there was no need for her to undertake that course because there would only be room for one farm manager in their future endeavours and it would be him. He advised her that she should study agribusiness and steer away from farm management. Fleur reluctantly agreed and changed her degree to agribusiness before moving to Victoria.

Fleur and Neil were married in the mid-nineties and soon after bought their own property, an 800-hectare block of land on the south coast of Western Australia. The farm had very few amenities, with just a shearing shed and a donga that they turned into their home. A 'donga' is a small demountable structure often used on construction sites as an office or temporary accommodation, but Fleur and Neil lived in this hut for seven years. It had holes in the walls, that Fleur used to stuff with steel wool to prevent mice getting in, and a shower that was accessed from outside. Their little home was a furnace in summer and a freezer in winter as the temperatures ranged from 10 degrees all the way up to 45 degrees throughout the seasons—and they felt every degree of it. In wild weather, the rain would hurl itself against the windows and the wind would shake the hut. For heating, Fleur would light the gas, open the oven door and try to take the chill off the air.

'We might as well have been living outside. I used to go to bed in a skivvy, a pair of tracksuit pants and a beanie. How I then got pregnant twice in 18 months, I don't know!'

To connect power to the hut was too expensive, so they ran a small petrol generator that gave them three hours of power each day, just enough time for Fleur to get some bookkeeping done on her computer and to put on a couple of loads of washing. Money was tight and they worked extremely hard to make ends meet while they grew their farming enterprise from the ground up. Fleur was actively involved in the running of the businesses both out in the paddock and in the office, managing their growing livestock and cropping operation. Fleur also craved a family and they soon welcomed little Rochelle into the world. The birth was traumatic for Fleur—a 36-hour labour resulted in some complications that required surgery, so Fleur remained in hospital for ten days before returning to the farm with her newborn. Adjusting to motherhood was a shock for Fleur, to say the least, and she experienced severe isolation during the early transition to becoming a mum. Her parents were unable to fly from South Australia due to a huge rain event that made access to their farm impassable for the first few weeks. Fleur had no one else to lean on for support.

'He [Neil] was off every day doing whatever he had to do on the farm and I had no one. I was pretty much left to my own devices. The isolation was crippling at times.'

But Fleur's challenges as a mother were only just beginning. Her geographical and social isolation was just the start of it. The sleep deprivation was gruelling and it was three months before Fleur finally felt well enough physically and mentally to work her way gently back to the farm work she'd been missing so much.

'I was in the sheep yards. Rochelle was in a pram that was chained up to the fence so she didn't tip over, and I suddenly felt really crook. I remember standing next to the sheep and vomiting up my two morning coffees thinking, oh God, last time I did this, I was pregnant.'

Rochelle was just a few months old when Fleur discovered she was pregnant again. The pregnancy was unplanned and especially challenging as Fleur was still recovering from the traumatic experience of her first birth. She grappled with feelings of frustration and guilt but tried to embrace this pregnancy as best as she could, hoping to have a smoother experience with her second child. Thirteen months after Rochelle's birth, Fleur welcomed her son Hayden into the world. And from there all hell broke loose.

'Those first few years with the kids are so foggy. All I can remember is neither of them slept, Rochelle didn't talk and Hayden just screamed.'

> I had no one. I was pretty much left to my own devices. The isolation was crippling at times.

As isolated as she was from family and friends, Fleur didn't know any many other mothers and no one was posting about their kids or parenting on social media as it just didn't exist at that time. Rochelle was a clumsy child, running into doors from time to time—small incidents that didn't ring any major alarm bells—and Fleur noticed that at nearly two years of age Rochelle still hadn't begun talking, but she brushed it off and didn't think much of it. However, during Rochelle's eighteen-month check-up, a nurse raised concern over the fact that she hadn't yet said her first word and referred Rochelle to a speech pathologist. The speech pathologist diagnosed Rochelle with verbal dyspraxia, a neurodevelopmental disorder that causes problems with movements of the mouth and tongue. Rochelle could understand her parents perfectly but she couldn't speak back to them. It wasn't until she was four years old that she finally started to communicate with words.

'We taught Rochelle Makaton sign language, which really helped us for a couple of years while she went through speech therapy. She's all grown up now and you can't shut her up!'

Fleur supported Rochelle's developmental needs through her toddler and preschool years, and this involved many hours of travel for therapy appointments. Baby Hayden was also showing signs of developmental challenges early on and his difficulties became more intense as he got older. He would scream for hours on end every day, and it soon became clear that his sensitivity was more than just that of a colicky infant. At two, Hayden wasn't yet walking, and he struggled with fine motor skills throughout his preschool years. One of the hardest things Fleur recalls was witnessing Hayden's extreme and distressing sensitivity to sounds.

'Our farm was on a flight path, and every time a jet flew over us Hayden would just stand there and bang his hands over his ears. Our dogs' barking drove him insane. If I got him into bed and there was a fly buzzing in his bedroom, he would just scream and scream and scream and scream until he went to sleep and would wake up screaming.'

Hayden was seven years old when he was finally diagnosed with autism. Autism is especially hard to identify in the early years of childhood because there are no medical tests and it's often impossible to rule out other developmental issues or disabilities. To help cope with each of their needs, Fleur taught both her children sign language and used that as a means of communicating. Looking after two children and living an isolated life on the farm was the hardest thing Fleur has ever done and something she probably doesn't give herself enough credit for. The emotional toll was significant, and she struggled with postnatal depression as she navigated those early years of motherhood. She sought professional help and started taking antidepressants, which lifted the fog and enabled her to find joy in her life again.

'It was a difficult time, but it built resilience and made me who I am today.

'I am so proud of both of my kids and all the challenges they have overcome throughout their lives.'

At this time when Fleur was physically and mentally depleted, she finally started to think about her own needs and how she could fill her own cup. Given Fleur's natural flair for English and writing, her parents had bought her a comprehensive writing course with no expiry date when she finished school, to nurture her undeniable talent. Fleur had always loved writing letters or short stories—as a teenager, it had been her way to express creativity without anyone else's input. However, between finishing school and having her children, Fleur hadn't written a word, and the writing course remained unused until after Hayden was born. Slowly, Fleur started to find ways to incorporate writing fiction into her life as a creative outlet for all the stress in her world. She crafted short stories for her children about farming, then she embarked on the writing course with the help of a long-distance tutor. Pretty soon she was hooked.

Fleur rediscovered her passion, writing snippets longhand on pieces of paper late at night in between tending to her children who were not good sleepers—in fact, she'd often give up on going to sleep herself. She would jot down notes and ideas when she was out moving sheep or sitting in the tractor during harvest. Whenever she had a rare moment of peace, Fleur was putting pen to paper and her tutor quickly recognised the amazing skill she had for storytelling. Fleur particularly enjoyed writing fiction where her protagonist was a strong woman working on a farm and, before she knew it, the stories were pouring out of her. By the way, Fleur never finished that long-distance writing course—she never had to.

In 2004, Fleur and her family purchased and moved into a newly built farmhouse on a neighbouring property. Soon after, they bought another block of land a few minutes' drive away, quickly building up their farming business to 3200 hectares, stocked with 10,000 ewes, 600 cows and a cropping enterprise. Fleur and Neil had come a long way since their donga days but, sadly, while their enterprise was growing, their marriage was crumbling. Alongside the pressure of raising two children with disabilities, largely on her own, Fleur had for many years also been dealing with the growing loneliness in her relationship with Neil. Writing was something that helped Fleur deal with the pressure, and in the end it proved a valuable investment of her time.

But Neil thought Fleur's writing was a waste of time. He regarded it as a silly hobby that he didn't want her to pursue. Yet ultimately, Fleur's determination to do whatever it took to follow her passion for writing is what eventually helped her to escape from her marriage.

She had saved up and secretly bought herself a laptop that she hid away from him. 'I'd write for as long as I could, running out to make sure there was no dust coming up the driveway, which would mean he was coming home. As soon as I heard him pull up, I'd shove my laptop under the bed, drop down to the ground and continue to fold laundry.'

When Fleur secured her first book deal—the opportunity of a lifetime—her confidence started to grow. Her writing tutor had encouraged her to reach out to a publisher and submit the first few chapters of a book she'd spent three years writing. This was *Red Dust*, and it told the tale of a young woman who defied all expectations and took on the management of a large station that her husband left to her after his tragic death in a plane crash—which turned out not to be an accident.

'I was sleep deprived and exhausted. I had these two screaming kids, I was still working on the farm and I have no idea where that storyline came from.'

The publisher loved it and offered Fleur a writing contract. In 2009, *Red Dust* was the highest-selling novel in Australia for a debut author. Fleur continued to write books, but she was completely unsupported by Neil.

'When I got that first writing contract, he told me that writing was something for a Sunday afternoon when all the other house and farm jobs had been done and that it wasn't any way to earn a living.'

As her writing career grew, so did the fear of leaving her twenty-year marriage. Her self-confidence had taken a battering. Fleur says she'd been thinking about leaving for a long time, but thinking and leaving are two different things.

I was sleep deprived and exhausted . . . I have no idea where that storyline came from.

Her lack of financial independence and a strong desire to stick it out for as long as possible for the kids was what made her stay. Then, in 2014, when Rochelle and Hayden were fourteen and thirteen, Fleur finally snapped and left. It's taken a lot of time and a lot of counselling, but it's a move she doesn't regret now.

'I got to the stage I couldn't handle the constant put-downs, and when I saw my children starting to use our relationship as a model for their behaviour, I knew I had to do something.'

At the time, Fleur was living three days a week in a house in town that she'd bought using a combination of her book royalties and small amount of farm income. Rochelle and Hayden attended high school there, and having a base meant they avoided the long daily commute back and forth from the farm. While they had a secure home and roof over their heads, Fleur still needed to find some long-term financial security and a handful of book deals wasn't going to cut it. She boldly called her publisher, explained her personal situation and committed to writing two books every year. The publisher agreed to the deal and the contracts and novels have kept coming ever since. When we caught up again in 2022, Fleur had finished her twentieth book and had sold more than 700,000 copies of her work worldwide.

Fleur has channelled her success for the greater good, pouring a lot of her money from her book sales into an organisation very close to her heart and one that gives back to the rural communities she loves. In 2017, she set up a not-for-profit called DVassist, which started as an online information directory of family and domestic violence services. It grew to offer anonymous and confidential online and phone counselling services for the regional areas of Western Australia, but unfortunately the new board was unable to secure government grants to grow the service and it has once again become an online directory and information service.

'When you live in the country, there's very little help for people experiencing domestic violence. But also people know your car, they can see if you're visiting a counsellor, there's no anonymity. It was important to me to create a confidential service. I do hope the counselling will start again very soon.'

Fleur has raised two incredibly strong and talented children who are now in their twenties. Rochelle left home a couple of years ago, while Hayden is making plans to move out in the coming months. This leaves Fleur to face uncharted territory in her motherhood journey and she admits she's struggling with the prospect.

'I'm about to become obsolete as a mum which is a very different feeling after everything we've been through and how much they've needed me in the past. It's a bit daunting.'

She won't have any trouble filling in her spare time though—she's already busy working on her 21st book. And while Fleur McDonald's novels tell the tales of strong rural women who defy the odds, not one is stronger than the author herself.

# 13

# Lyn Kelson: No goodbye

## Drummond, Victoria

When Lyn Kelson and I catch up, my face is a little red and swollen because I've been crying. A cattle ear tag with the number 411 sits on my desk next to me, a heartbreaking reminder of the little mate I lost earlier that day. Tiddler (named by Elliot) was a four-month-old calf I'd hand-raised after we saved him from death's door when he was a newborn. But that morning I had found him dead. There had been no warning signs; it was sudden, it was shocking and it was inexplicable. Yesterday he had been a happy and healthy animal and I adored him.

Tiddler's death was a startling reminder for me that life is short but during my video call with Lyn I felt silly explaining my grief over the death of a calf because Lyn's life has been full of unimaginable loss. The pain Lyn has endured and survived throughout her 54 years would have broken most people, but not Lyn; she truly is one of the kindest and strongest women I've ever met. Her life changed in an instant after the suicide of her first love, her husband Kevin, and it cruelly spiralled into more heartache throughout her life.

'There is a huge amount of guilt. And everybody has the same questions, asking me as his wife what happened to him. Why did he do that? And I haven't got the answers either.'

Lyn was one of six children and grew up in the tiny town of Tylden in central Victoria. She lived in an old house that still had an outside kitchen and a dairy room, but the highlight was an underground cellar, a special place of sanctuary she'd sneak away to as a little girl and devour book after book. She lived on a small hobby farm with sheep and horses, but their family's property quickly grew into a small shelter for animals. Lyn's father had worked as a Fisheries and Wildlife officer early on in his career and was constantly rescuing and rearing injured possums and koalas. As a child, Lyn's love for animals and the environment was inspired by her nurturing dad.

'My dad was my mainstay through everything in my life, the good and the bad. He was a very good man.'

Lyn reflects fondly on her father. He was an avid cyclist and would take Lyn and her siblings to cycling tracks, local races and to compete in meets across their region. Lyn's sister Heather went on to be a national cycling champion and her brother competed overseas. Lyn loved the sport, although her interests were soon drawn elsewhere.

Lyn finished school at seventeen, left home to pursue a career in nursing and was accepted into a three-year hospital-based education program (the equivalent of university education today). She moved to Melbourne's north and took up her training position at Preston and Northcote Community Hospital in Preston, and it's there she discovered her passion for caring for people, particularly in palliative care as they prepared for the end of their life. During her second year of nursing, she fell head over heels for Kevin Condon, a young man she'd met through friends. Lyn was a shy young woman but this new crush of hers, Kevin, was very different. He was confident and outspoken but warm with a great sense of humour, and he made everyone who knew him laugh. He and his friends were involved with the local footy club which is where Lyn got her first taste of his urban world.

'I was a country girl. All these other women at the footy club were city people and talked about their nails and make-up and fashion. My clothes came from op shops and I had my own sort of style.'

Despite coming from very different worlds, Kevin and Lyn hit it off and their relationship blossomed quickly. Kevin was a welder by trade and when he and Lyn first met he was building sets for the Victorian State Opera, so many of their courting days were spent going on dates together in Melbourne, enjoying opera productions and indulging their shared love of classical music. As a young country girl, Lyn was enamoured with the bright lights and excitement of live theatre. Kevin and Lyn also shared a love for nature and spent a lot of time together camping and exploring the beach and the bush. In 1988, less than a year after they first met, Lyn and Kevin were walking along the Lerderderg Gorge near Bacchus Marsh in Victoria when they stopped to sit on a log for a rest and a chat. Kevin suddenly became very quiet, and, concerned, Lyn asked him if he was all right then moments later, he turned to her and proposed, asking 'Lyn, do you think you'd want to be Mrs Condon?' Of course, she said yes.

Kevin and Lyn got married on 14 October 1989, at St Bernard's Church in Bacchus Marsh. Kevin came from a traditional Catholic family, so the newlyweds hadn't lived together prior to exchanging their vows. But shortly after they wed and began their life together, they bought a tiny brown brick veneer house in the small town of Myrniong in Victoria. It was a two-bedroom home, just 85 square metres in size, but it sat on a half-acre block with adjoining farmland. Lyn didn't want for much else in her life at the time, except for the laughter of children to fill their home—she always dreamed of a big brood. Not long after she and Kevin were married, she fell pregnant with their first child, a little girl they named Emily who was born in January 1991. Twenty months later, they welcome their son Christiaan into the world.

'We'd go down to the creek and have picnics. Life felt just perfect when we lived there. We had our two kids, and there were only two bedrooms, so the kids squashed into one bedroom together.'

Lyn thrived as a new mum over the first couple of years but she challenged Kevin's traditional family beliefs around women's roles. He'd come from a line of females who were all stay-at-home mums. But Lyn was a different kettle of fish and was an anomaly in his family, returning to work as a nurse when Emily was nine months old. Lyn's passion for helping people was unstoppable, and after receiving her full nursing qualifications she decided to work in palliative care, looking after people in their homes during their final months of life. Her mother-in-law came around to the idea that her daughter-in-law was a working mum and she gave Lyn a lot of support, taking care of the kids several afternoons a week. Lyn remembers the juggle well. She'd pop home whenever she could during her shifts to breastfeed before heading back to work. Lyn loved her job but there were also growing financial pressures that meant her nursing career ensured much needed additional income for their growing family.

'Things were tight enough on our household budget as it was, but at the time interest rates were ridiculous, so we had a significant financial burden to carry even with our tiny little house. It was quite difficult to maintain financial viability.'

Kevin worked as a fabrication welder at an engineering firm in town, and in spite of the financial strain Lyn believes they were both quite happy, or so she thought. Lyn was frugal, ensuring they stuck to their weekly budget by preserving food and cooking all their meals, knitting and making clothes for the family. She adored her children, revelled in motherhood and was grateful for the loving home that she and Kevin had built together.

'I was very much in love with Kevin throughout that time, and, you know, I thought we were doing well.'

The day started like any other day when Kevin went off to work on the morning of 18 November 1994. It wasn't uncommon for him to work long hours and come home late. He was working overtime some evenings and sometimes enjoyed popping to the gym on his way home to Lyn and the kids. However by 9 pm, after Lyn had fed the kids and put them to bed, Kevin still wasn't home, and Lyn felt something shift inside her. Her intuition was telling her something wasn't quite right. Mobile phones were expensive and uncommon back then so she couldn't simply call him, but just sitting and waiting for him to walk through the door wasn't an option either. So, she bundled a sleepy three-year-old Emily and two-year-old Christiaan into her car and ventured off into the night.

> . . . we had a significant financial burden to carry even with our tiny little house.

Lyn drove straight to Kevin's workplace a few kilometres away. When she arrived, she spotted Kevin's car parked out the front near the sheds. She had to scale the fence into the compound. The door to one of the sheds was ajar. She opened it and looked around by torch light but there was no sign of Kevin inside. The other shed nearby was locked so she called Kevin's boss from a streetside phone box and he agreed to meet her there and help with the search. He arrived with the keys to the second shed and what Lyn saw when they unlocked it and walked inside will haunt her forever. As the fluorescent lights flickered on in the workshop, she saw Kevin hanging by a rope from the rafters. The ladder that he'd stepped off was next to him. In the office, he'd left a note.

'I still know virtually every word of that note. It's amazing how it gets seared into your brain. I was in shock. It's an experience I wish no one ever had to live through.'

Emily and Christiaan continued to sleep peacefully in the car outside, oblivious to the heartache that their mum was enduring when the police arrived. The days that followed were a blur for Lyn as she dealt with the cruel reality of being widowed at the age of 26. Planning Kevin's funeral and picking out his coffin are still some of the most bizarre things she's ever done in her life, and when it came time to say goodbye at his funeral, the weight of her loss hit her like a sledgehammer. So much so that she couldn't bring herself to go to Kevin's wake and face the crowds of people from the community who had shown up to farewell him. Lyn just wanted to lock the doors and shut herself and her kids off from the rest of the world. And she did just that, for as much time as she could.

'It took me a long time to stick my head out in public again. And it's really weird when you have to go back into society because people can't look at you the same anymore.'

When Lyn now reflects on Kevin's sudden death, she still has no answers. There were no warning signs and over the years she has grown tired of the constant questions that at times have seemed accusatory, asking why Kevin took his own life. Struggling with her grief, she tried to be the best possible mother to her two little children, who would ask, 'Mummy, why isn't Daddy coming home?' Lyn's pain was excruciating and she focused on simply surviving. The community rallied behind her and financial support came in thick and fast as locals did what they could to support them. She and Keven had been half way through a renovation, and it was completed and paid for by the generosity of the community and an outpouring of love that helped Lyn through the most traumatic time of her life.

Mummy, why isn't Daddy coming home?

'I probably wasn't the best mother I could be, given the circumstances. It wasn't what I imagined motherhood was going to be. I thought I would have a tribe of kids and we'd be happy, go on whacky holidays and build beautiful memories. But that's not what happened. I've really not got many memories from those years because I was just surviving.'

Lyn says that for the first few months after losing Kevin, all she wanted to do was shrivel up and die, but her children gave her purpose and were the reason she kept going. Over time, she sought counselling, which helped her work through her grief so she could shed the guilt she had been carrying since Kevin's suicide. Slowly, she prepared to rebuild her life from the ground up and find herself again. She decided to sell the family home, a move she struggled with as the tight-knit local community had given her so much support and she didn't want to seem ungrateful by packing up and leaving the area. However, the memories were too painful, and she needed a fresh start. Her parents supported her financially so she could buy a house closer to them so they could help her. It was a charming old Victorian house that came with a bit of land, so Lyn and the kids got a house cow, some chickens and a veggie patch, restarting their self-sufficiency journey, a constant theme through Lyn's life on the land.

Lyn was reluctant to jump into the dating game during this period, but she was also incredibly lonely and missing connection. She had met a nurse called Matthew while she was still working at the Bacchus Marsh hospital and decided to give him a chance. He relocated with her and the children when they moved into their new home, and things went well initially. But when they started discussing their future more seriously, they hit a roadblock. Lyn was aspiring to become a doctor and had applied to study medicine in Sydney. This would involve her sitting an exam and, if she passed, she planned to make the move to the big smoke. Matthew wasn't keen on this idea and didn't want to relocate to the city, so their relationship hit a stalemate. But before they could work through their issues and decide whether they still had a future together, disaster struck.

Early in the morning of 25 March 1998, Lyn had just finished a night shift at the hospital when she returned home and plonked down onto the bed. Bleary-eyed and sleeping with one eye open, she tried to rest as much as she could while six-year-old Emily and four-year-old Christiaan played in the house. Suddenly, they ran inside and told her they could see a big orange helicopter from the backyard. Lyn sprang out of bed and ran to the back door where she saw an Elvis chopper sucking water out of the dam over her back fence. The unmistakable glow of fire and smoke blanketed the sky and, although Lyn didn't know it at the time, a fierce blaze was aggressively making its way towards her home.

The sparks travelling ahead of the blaze created a fireball that was raging closer and spitting ash and embers into Lyn's yard.

'I thought shit, I've got to get myself organised. I immediately started going around with a wet towel trying to put out the sparks but soon surrendered to the fact that it was a bad idea because you could see this fire was moving too quickly.'

In a panic, Lyn picked up the most recent basket of washing, a loaf of bread, her jewellery box and a bag of apples, asking Emily and Christiaan to grab a toy and the woollen blanket off their beds. Lyn raced out to let her chickens free, grabbing her dogs and her cat and piling her kids and their pets into the car. By then, the fire was already at their back door.

'As we were driving away, the house virtually blew up. I watched over my shoulder as it burned and drove straight to the nearest evacuation site.'

The next day, Lyn returned to find nothing left of her home apart from the old stone chimney and piles of ash and twisted up iron. Emily was in Grade 1 and Christiaan was in Prep at the time, and suddenly they were all homeless with nothing much to keep them going but a few changes of clothes. Precious items perished in the blaze, but she managed to save her wedding album and two photo albums with photos of Kevin that she had made up for Emily and Christiaan, a small blessing amid the cruel loss.

'Shit happens and you can't change it, that's what I've learned. It doesn't pay to be angry and sad because you can't change the past. I can't bring back dead people. I can't undo a bushfire. I can only go forward.'

Lyn moved in with her mother immediately after the fire and stayed with her for two weeks until she was able to get back on her feet. She also broke things off with Matthew and was determined to make her way to Sydney to study medicine. Just a few days after the blaze, Lyn had to sit the medical entrance exam she'd been studying hard for. Her heart was aching after losing her home and she was worried about how she was going to support her children and give them some normality after everything they'd been through over the years. To say she was distracted as she sat the exam would be an understatement. Devastatingly, Lyn missed the entry score by just two marks, and she was denied any concession for her recent losses. Within a week, she had lost both her home and her dream of becoming a doctor, but she just kept going.

> Shit happens and you can't change it, that's what I've learned . . . I can't bring back dead people. I can't undo a bushfire. I can only go forward.

A year later, in 1999, Lyn, Emily and Christiaan had settled into life in their new home in Trentham when Lyn decided to change the direction of her career. She completed her graduate diploma of midwifery and began working as a midwife at Daylesford Hospital, and her desire for more children was reignited. Soon after, she met a man called Mark (not his real name), introduced to her by a few of her local friends. Mark was a corporate accountant who'd recently moved down from Sydney, and very quickly he and Lyn became romantically involved. Just three months after meeting, they unexpectedly fell pregnant and they went on to have two children together, a girl, Estelle, and a boy, Sebastian, in late 2000 and early 2002. Unfortunately, their relationship only lasted six years before Lyn called it quits when things took a toxic turn.

'I persisted with that relationship for a very long time because I didn't want two more kids with no dad, and I didn't want to be a failure again. There was a whole heap of reasons why things eventually fell apart.'

Unlucky in love, Lyn once again found herself alone and in a dire financial situation with four children to support. It was then that she thought back to her childhood and her powerful connection to the land and animals. Deep down, she realised she wanted to be a farmer and own a large block of land that would bring in additional income and also be a place of safety and solitude—her forever home after so much instability.

Lyn started her farming journey by purchasing a farm at Spring Hill and there's been no stopping her since. She worked her way up to 50 breeding cows, selling the calves to market, reinvesting the money in the property and saving for a rainy day. She's a self-proclaimed, self-taught farmer who learned to run the property on her own with little experience, few skills and next to nothing in her bank account after her relationship with Mark left her high and dry. She found a way to farm that doesn't apply conventional chemicals or fertilisers, initially because she simply couldn't afford them but since then because she's fallen in love with regenerative agriculture, which focuses on natural farming methods that improve soil health and biodiversity. Lyn kept the farm running productively on her own, continuing her work as a midwife and raising four kids. In 2005, she completed her master's degree in midwifery when her youngest two were just five and four years old.

'And because I believe that life should be full of love, I actually partnered up again soon after that. I had another fella because—in the spirit of Beccy Cole—rather than needing to be a better woman, I needed a better man!'

That fella is Phil. Lyn and he met in 2008 through an online dating site and they've been together ever since. Phil is a mechanical engineer who grew up in the country, and in 2010 he and Lyn bought a 65-hectare farm together in the town of Drummond. They now run 30 breeding cows and 80 sheep on what Lyn hopes will be her forever home. In addition to operating their farming business and getting her hands dirty, Lyn has also found her sweet spot in maternal health as a birth educator. She runs her own mentoring business that supports women to have empowered births, leaning on her decades of experience as a midwife and, of course, finding inspiration from the most rewarding role of her life as mum to her four kids. Lyn's passion for motherhood is evident in her voice as we speak on the phone and she brings me up to speed on what Emily, Christiaan, Estelle and Sebastian are all up to. Lyn has had a few years of an empty nest at home and now the constant chaos of kids has been replaced with the calm of the country.

On an average day, you'll find Lyn sitting on her hill, looking down across her farm towards Mount Macedon, soaking in the silence. She tells me this is her solace, her favourite place in the world. Reflecting on her 54 years, so much of Lyn's life has been spent grieving loss after loss and coping with constant instability but Lyn's strength is remarkable. The past decade on the land has finally enabled her to connect more with herself and has given her the slower pace of life she desperately needed. In so many ways, the land has healed her.

'Every day is a gift and you have to be accountable for what you do with every day. There are days I choose to do nothing but I *choose* that. I choose to sit in the sun and watch the leaves fall or whatever it is. I don't choose to be racing around aimlessly trying to achieve shit for other people and I don't need to impress anybody else these days. I live for me.'

# 14

# Diana Butler: From Tasmania to remote Tanzania

## Launceston, Tasmania

Music is blaring in the background. Diana Butler and I are deep in conversation in the corner of a room at my sister-in-law's wedding reception, chatting business goals and the meaning of life—you know, just the kind of light conversation you'd expect to have at a party. Diana has been a close friend of the Trethewey family for many years, but it's only in the past few months that the two of us have started to get to know each other and form our own special connection.

During our post-nuptial chat, I realised just how little I knew about Diana's personal story, a story filled with unimaginable pain and grief as well as incredible grit and determination.

After a roller-coaster of a journey on and off the land, Diana now dedicates her life to helping others, supporting some of the world's poorest people—a mission that began sixteen years ago when a trip to Africa changed her life forever. Diana is one of those rare people who doesn't just show immense empathy when faced with other people's pain but actively rolls up her sleeves to do something about it. Tens of thousands of people in Tanzania are grateful for that.

'I remember I was standing under a tree and I broke down and I said, "I can't do this. This is just all too much. Where do you start?" And then something deep inside my core said, "Diana, stand up, make a difference." So I stood up and I said to the people that I would help them, and from that moment on I have honoured my commitment.'

Diana grew up in the rural community of Hollow Tree in the Central Highlands of Tasmania on her parents' sheep and cattle farm. She shared being the youngest with her twin brother and they had two older brothers. As the only girl, she says she lived within the confines of a patriarchal society and life on the land, especially back then, was dominated by men. There was a loneliness in Diana's childhood, and she worked with her mum a lot, helping her with house chores, particularly cooking meals for her father and three brothers. Over the years, she watched the men in her family with awe and envy each day as they headed out on the property to work. She longed to be part of their farming world but she had been taught that her role was inside the home not out in the paddocks or sheep yards.

'I used to think, "Why can't I do that? What's wrong with me?" I didn't understand what was wrong with me until I worked out that I couldn't go with them because I was a girl. So I used to pray at night that I'd turn into a boy.'

Diana spent a lot of her childhood alone and would often retreat to the garden on the farm where she played imaginary games with imaginary people. She describes it as living in a fantasy world where she would help people in faraway lands, looking after them and mothering them. In many ways, Diana's future script was written right there and then. In the years that followed, she decided she would become a nurse when she finished school, a path her mother and her grandmother had taken before her and a career that turned her fantasy into reality.

Despite Diana's ambition to become a nurse, she was a quiet and timid teen in Year 7 when she headed off to an all-girls boarding school in Hobart. When she began her high school journey, she struggled to find her confidence but by the time she graduated Year 12 Diana was flourishing and her self-esteem had skyrocketed, thanks to the support of her teachers and peers. Surrounded by other strong young women, Diana realised that she was far more capable than she had imagined.

After finishing school, Diana began a three-and-a-half-year traineeship to become a registered nurse, just as she'd planned. But during her studies, at nineteen years of age, Cupid's arrow struck and Diana was whisked off her feet by a strapping young farmer she'd met one weekend at a rural black-tie party. That party changed everything and three years later, at the tender age of 22, Diana married that man and moved to his family farm of grazing and cropping country in Tassie's Northern Midlands. Diana was thrust back into rural life, determined to dedicate herself to farm life and family life, putting her personal goals and nursing career aspirations on the backburner for nearly two decades.

'That's when my work as a nurse in town started dropping away. I was consumed by country life. I became very competent at cooking scones, lunches and morning tea. It was very much a man's world and I was always the dutiful wife that looked after and cared for my husband.'

At 24, Diana fell pregnant with their first child and she was overjoyed. After a wonderful pregnancy, she recalls with some humour the moment on the farm when her waters broke. She raced to tell her husband, who was in the sheep yards, and had to persuade him that it was time to leave the livestock and drive her to the hospital. Diana was excited to become a mother but once her little boy Tom was born, her joy turned to heartbreak. After a complex delivery, Diana held her newborn son for just a few seconds before he was whisked off to intensive care. She knew something was very wrong. Baby Tom had a diaphragmatic hernia, a birth defect which occurs when there is a hole in the diaphragm, the thin sheet of muscle that separates the chest from the abdomen, meaning he was unable to breathe on his own because his lungs were underdeveloped. Doctors in Launceston planned to send Tom to Melbourne where they had a specialist team ready to operate but he just wasn't strong enough to make the trip. Their next option was Hobart but Tom didn't make it. He lived for just nine hours before he passed away in Diana's arms.

'Thirty-six years later, there is not a day that I don't think of my Tom, and even talking about it makes me want to weep. It is the hardest thing in life that I have ever done, to give the child away that I gave birth to. It is part of who you are. I did a lot of soul-searching. I lost all faith and all hope in life and I know what it's like to hit rock bottom.'

> There is not a day that I don't think of my Tom, and even talking about it makes me want to weep . . .

When Diana came back home to the farm, the cruel blows continued. She was given medication to suppress her milk production but for the first week she'd wake up with breasts full of milk, longing to feed her baby. Diana clung to the photos she'd taken of Tom and to his ashes, which she'd brought home with her and which she travels with to this day. During those raw first few months of intense grief, Diana felt incredibly isolated. No one knew what to say to her or how to help. She even recalls a woman she knew very well crossing the road in town after seeing her, to avoid any interaction or discussion with her.

'I do remember one night—it's clear as a bell. I had a glass of whisky. And another one. And another one. And I slept that night and the pain was gone. And I looked at the bottle of whisky the next morning and I thought, if I have a glass of whisky that pain will go, but look what will become of me. It gave me a real insight into how people can become alcoholics.'

Diana largely suffered in silence and didn't seek professional support—mental health and dealing with trauma were taboo topics at that time. What did help heal some of her wounds was becoming pregnant with her second baby, another little boy. This child was the biggest blessing for Diana after the pain she'd been through, but her confidence was shaken and she was terrified of losing him too. She'd have nightmares that he wouldn't survive during her pregnancy, but after nine long months and a complication-free labour, Ben, or 'Booie' as he's affectionately called, was born happy and healthy. The relief Diana felt was intense and she thrived through early motherhood, eager to grow her family further. Nineteen months later, Diana and her husband welcomed another healthy boy called John, fondly known as Johno. Three years after that, another son, Harry, was born. Diana says the early days of being a young mum were bliss. She adored being a mother and she devoted her life to her sons and to her role managing the domestic work.

Crucially, Diana kept working as a nurse in town half a day a week, which was all she needed to in order to maintain her registration. As her three boys got older and more independent, Diana became restless. She felt confined inside the home being a dutiful housewife and yearned to break free and pursue some of her professional dreams. Whenever she could find the time amid the chaos of raising three boys, Diana would lose herself in books, biographies of women to be exact, devouring story after story about strong women who were leading incredible lives. She read books about missionaries and colonies and became engrossed in learning how dysfunctional foreign aid can sometimes be in developing countries. Her knowledge ignited a passion and sowed the seed of an idea in her mind—perhaps there was something more for her out there beyond the farm gate.

'Look, to be quite honest, I did struggle because I wanted more in life. I loved bringing my children up on the farm: it brought me so much joy. I threw myself into gardening; there was quite a community around and we looked after each other, but I didn't have the opportunity to express this deeper side of myself. There was no room for the expansion of my mind and I hungered for that.'

Sadly, when her youngest son Harry was nine years old, Diana's marriage fell apart. When she and her husband separated, Diana had the heart-wrenching task of leaving the land with her three boys to start a new life as a single mum in town. It was a bittersweet moment but it finally enabled Diana to go on and live the life that she wanted. She rented a little house, juggled her three boys and focused on her future career aspirations. At the age of 39, she started studying for a Bachelor of Nursing and overcame numerous obstacles, including the fact that when she first started her course, Diana didn't know how to type on a computer and used to pay someone to do it for her! She says one of the proudest moments of her life was not just overcoming those hurdles and completing her degree but having her three sons by her side at her graduation.

'I was so proud to shift their mindset around their mother—that I wasn't just a farmer's wife, that I had my own identity. I wanted to break that cycle.'

When Diana secured full-time work as an emergency nurse at the local hospital, it was exhilarating for her; she finally felt like she was carving her own path, but it was tough. She worked night shifts and admits she often only slept about four hours a night or day for several years, struggling to keep up with the pressures of her career and the responsibilities of motherhood. At one point, Diana was heading to work at the hospital at 9.30 pm and not getting home until 7.30 am the next morning. Then she'd get her boys up and take them to school before getting a few precious hours of sleep. Occasionally she would head to her second job at a GP surgery straight after working a night shift, working until 3pm and saving that extra money for their groceries. When the sleep deprivation got too much and too dangerous, Diana pulled back to just her hospital work and by then she'd worked hard to be financially independent and could provide her boys with the life in town that she wanted for them.

In 2006, Diana's life and future trajectory changed forever. While working a shift at the hospital one day she spoke with a young doctor from Africa who had a scholarship to study medicine in Australia. The doctor told Diana a compelling story about her father who had established a small, 34-bed hospital in a remote part of Tanzania in an effort to support his community. He would often have to operate by candlelight because the hospital had no electricity or running water. Diana heard this story and immediately wanted to help. She gathered a group of nursing colleagues and organised a fundraiser to purchase and send medical supplies to the Tanzanian hospital. With the money raised, Diana bought a generator, which was transported to Tanzania in a shipping container also filled with donated hospital equipment, including hospital beds, an electrocardiogram machine, bandages, masks, syringes and a blood fridge.

It took around six weeks for that container to make the 11,000-kilometre journey from Tasmania to Tarime in Tanzania. Diana wasn't content with the send-off and wanted to escort the supplies to their new home and see for herself the impact they would have. Along with her colleague the late Dr Peter Hewitt and his daughter Emma, she flew to Africa on what Diana describes a 'fact-finding mission'. The moment they arrived in the first outlying rural community of Tarime, they were swamped by a sea of people and immediately Diana saw things that she could never unsee or forget. The extreme poverty was devastating. The local people were unable to access basic health care or clean drinking water. When it came to medical support, there were only three qualified doctors in the region for a population the same size as the whole of Tasmania.

'After that trip, I couldn't walk away from those people. I came back home and said to my team, "We've got to help these people and we're going to start by sending them an ambulance!"'

Some might have thought she was dreaming but after an incredible fundraising effort, Diana and her team of dedicated emergency nurses and volunteers managed to acquire an Ambulance Tasmania vehicle that was sent over in a second shipment to Tanzania. I've seen the photo of the ambulance loaded in the shipping container and it's quite extraordinary to think about the journey it made. Packed inside the ambulance were educational and medical aids that were distributed to the hospital and to the community in poverty-stricken Tarime. This extraordinary effort and generosity marked the launch of the community's first mobile health clinic, but Diana wasn't done.

I came back home and said to my team,
'We've got to help these people . . .'

Later that year, together with Dr Peter Hewitt, she founded Care for Africa Foundation a charity that now works extensively with the people of Tarime, focusing on fostering growth and self-sufficiency in communities, through clean water, health, education and economic wellbeing. As CEO, Diana has led Care for Africa into a pioneering organisation that to date has installed twelve deep-water bores to bring clean water to 32,000 people. The water bores are installed at schools and community collection points, as well as at the hospital.

'We put a water bore in a school and it increases school attendance from 68 per cent to 90 per cent. Most of the girls spend their days collecting water so they can't attend school and as a result are trapped in the cycle of poverty. A water bore at the local school allows girls freedom of life beyond just collecting water.'

Diana helped establish the Care for Africa breakfast program that now feeds over 6000 schoolchildren every day, ensuring they're not going to school on empty stomachs and can maintain their energy levels throughout the day. Diana is particularly passionate about empowerment programs that educate, upskill and provide business opportunities for women and girls across Tarime. She also sponsors women's groups, setting them up with the equipment to make soap. During the COVID-19 pandemic, the water bores and handmade soap were the only real sanitation products available to protect the community.

A water bore at the local school allows girls freedom of life beyond just collecting water.

Under Diana's leadership, Care for Africa has also established a Rural School Mobile Health Clinic, which runs annually in eight community schools, built a primary school and created social enterprise programs that focus on the empowerment of women. In 2016, she was made a Member of the Order of Australia for her humanitarian work in Tanzania. Her focus now is to grow the charity's reach in Africa, and her long-term dream is to develop an international model for sustainable foreign aid that will give independence, control and self-sufficiency to people in poverty. It is the voice of the people and the ear that listens that enables change—in other words, the change must come from the people who are living in the situation. The communities know exactly what they need. She's designing the system to ensure that communities can thrive without being at the mercy of foreign aid and donations. That model, Diana says, will be her legacy.

It's been seventeen years since Diana founded the charity. Over those years, she's devoted so much of herself to her three boys, to her career and to the people of Africa. During that time she also managed to find a precious gift that she'd been craving since leaving the farm all those years ago—love. Diana connected with a man named Nick when she was on a skiing trip with her children. Nick was also divorced and had children of his own. The pair became very close friends and it took a couple of years before they got together. Diana in particular approached their relationship with trepidation—after all, they had five children between them to think about.

'We were in a lift in Melbourne and I actually said to Nick, "I don't think I can do a proper relationship. I've got my life in Africa and I will not be a good partner to you. No one can clip my wings." And he said, "Trust me, I'll help you fly". I will always remember those words and I think from that moment on, I've never looked back.'

Just shy of her 50th birthday, Diana married Nick in an intimate ceremony with five guests present—their children. As for her three (now adult) boys, Diana couldn't be more proud. Ben, 'Booie', is back on the land farming in Tasmania on his father's property, happily partnered to Kirsty and has since had two sons of his own. Johno is also based in Tassie, married to Molly and with a son and daughter. Johno works as a project manager within the power industry. Harry lives in Sydney and has taken after Diana in many ways, setting up his own consultancy business working with First Nations communities in Australia.

Reflecting on her time as a mother both on and off the land, Diana can't help but think of the Tanzanian women and mothers she's connected with over the years. They may be poor, she tells me, but in many ways they are far richer than many of us who are mothering in the western world. There is more loneliness here. The isolation and the pressures that come with parenthood in the developed world can be overwhelming. It really does take a village to raise a child and it takes a community of people to support the wellbeing of a mother too. You only need to turn to Tanzania to see how well they understand that. It's no surprise that Diana has fallen in love with the culture and the people who offer each other so much love and support despite their circumstances.

'There is community and there is joy. And I see children running down the street with no toys but they connect with each other. In our community, there's a disconnect. We have IT and all these sophisticated systems to keep us together but there is a breakdown in our society. Whereas in Tanzania, life is simple and they help raise each other's children. There is that communal base and community is so important.'

The adversity Diana has faced on her motherhood journey and her fight to find her purpose off the land have made her who she is today. It'd be hard to find a more doting mum and grandmother than Diana and her optimism is infectious. She's truly one of the most beautiful people I've ever had the pleasure of knowing. I admire the way in which her painful past hasn't defined her but rather it has propelled her forward with a fierce sense of gratitude. I think we could all use a little bit of Diana in our lives, someone to remind us that it is possible to harness our greatest challenges and, instead of wallowing in self-pity, use them to create meaningful change not just for ourselves but for others too.

'I'm a great believer that our pains become our gifts. If we work through them, we can learn so much about humanity and we can go out into the world, into our community, wherever, and give back to people who are suffering.'

# Epilogue

From time to time, I ponder how very different my life would be now if I'd never left the city. I know that in many ways I'd be a different woman and perhaps a different mother. That slow news day when 'just another interview' turned out to be the most consequential interview of my journalistic life led me here. Home.

The silver lining of the paralysing isolation I have felt both geographically and socially over the past few years is this: it has removed all the unnecessary distractions from my life, all the outside noise. Life on the land has forced me to face my fears and face myself. Turns out solitude can be a humbling and transformational experience if you let it. Walking away from the rat race and my city career allowed me to run my own race for the first time in my life and gave me the opportunity to find out what really makes me tick—and that's connecting with rural mothers. I have found my people.

There is no doubt that I have changed. Rural life has seen me turn my back on many of the consumables that once consumed me and I feel myself surrendering more deeply to this life as the weeks pass. I rarely wear make-up, most of my 'city' clothes are in storage collecting dust and my daily outfit (whether I'm in the office or on the farm) is a pair of jeans and a work shirt, often stained with cow shit or grease. And I'm more than okay with that. While I no longer dine at fancy restaurants and I can't get food delivered to my door, I am more connected to my food than I have ever been. If you drive up to our homestead on any given day at lunchtime, you might even catch a glimpse of me in our veggie garden—a newfound passion that would be inconceivable to the 'old Steph'. Granted, I'm doing a better job of killing plants than actually growing them at the moment but I am learning and there have been few things more rewarding than cooking a meal for my family with our home-grown vegetables and our home-grown meat. This life is intoxicating and grounding and I am hooked.

When it comes to motherhood, I am still finding my feet. Do we ever? But when it all becomes too much, when the thought of leaving the house, seeing people or doing anything beyond the bare minimum with two young kids sends my head into a spin, we simply stay here. In our safe place. With hundreds of hectares at our doorstep. And they're here with me too, an increasingly vocal community of rural mums, a club I feel privileged to be a member of.

There's no doubt that Motherland is my third child. Just like my two children, I have grown it, nurtured it and worked hard to keep it alive and thriving. And while as Sam would eloquently put it 'our breeding days are over' (and I 1000 per cent concur), this baby of mine, Motherland, is just getting started.

# My *Motherland* musings

## Addicted

It's the strangest thing, this farm bubble of ours.
There are days I yearn to burst it.

Life on the land has consumed our little family.
We live where we work. We work where we live.

They cry out at 6 am, and the day begins.
Work. Emails. Phone calls.
Laundry. Cooking. Cleaning.
Playtime. Bath time. Bedtime.

And repeat.

Day after day, he heads out, while I stay in.
He's often just a few hundred metres away,
but he still feels so far away.
Will it always be this way?

I miss our weekends. The spontaneous, pre-kids,
city-based, sleep-in kind.
Now, Saturdays and Sundays still have that Monday-to-Friday feel.

Farm work never stops.
I wish he could knock off.
I wish we could both clock off.

So I was surprised that when I left our little bubble,
and headed to the city for the first time in over a year,
I didn't feel free.
I didn't feel invigorated.

I missed the farm.
I missed the stillness.
I missed the land.

So I think I'm addicted to our bubble . . .

Despite all it demands.

## My love

He's my calm in chaos.
My safe place.
My home.

Once upon a time, my phone was filled with photos of him.
And only him.
But today, I find myself scrolling back through months of baby snaps before I finally find his gorgeous face.

Last night, I cried because I miss him so much.
We can lose ourselves in motherhood, but for some of us, the hardest loss of all can be this . . . him.
Just the two of you. It's okay to grieve that.

Like so many rural dads, he works so damn hard.
He floats in and out.
Mostly out.
While I'm here.
Grinding it out at home.

I beam when I hear his ute pull up every night.
I sigh when he leaves in the morning.

And weekends. What are those?
It never stops. He never stops.
The farm needs him.
But so do I.

Life on the land sets his soul on fire.
He's exactly where he's meant to be.
And now I know, so am I.

But this season we're in, is one of the hardest.
We're raising two littles ones.
Looking after them.
Looking after the farm.
But not always looking after us.

But when our world pauses, for just a moment, we're reminded
that we are each other's world.
There are quick pecks on the lips and cuddles I wish
would linger longer . . .
But when the kids are tucked away, and we finally let go of the
stresses of the day, we always find our way back to each other for
those precious moments. That kiss.
And that's how I know,
We got this.

## Groundhog day

It can be lonely here on the land sometimes can't it, Mama?
It's home, it's our haven, but it can feel like groundhog day.
The weeks seem like they roll into one.

The days are long, wrangling the kids.
Our partners are out working. Rarely around.
You finally get your little ones to bed,
and then you get 'that' text . . .

'I'll be home late. Sorry, darling. I've had a
problem with the seeder.'

It feels like a big slap in the face. Even though it's not his fault.
You were looking forward to seeing him. Having a glass
of wine together. Catching up.
How odd it is to miss someone you live with.

Bloody hell, having a 9–5 'normal' job feels like
your family's dream sometimes.

Perhaps it's been weeks since you last saw any
neighbours or friends.
They might be hours away, or they might just be up the road.
You crave a change of scenery, but the thought of packing the
kids in the car and going into town on your own seems
like too much hassle.

It's easier to stay here. So you do.

Perhaps you're geographically isolated.
Or perhaps you feel lonely even with the closest town not far away.

Motherhood can swallow you up, Mama.
And while rural life is so God-damn beautiful, it requires strength,
especially during a time when we are at our most fragile.
We are so desperately in need of support. A village.

You're doing an amazing job, you know? With those
beautiful kids of yours . . .
Maybe no one is around to see it. Maybe you feel alone,
But you are far from it.

## My Akubra

I wear this hat,
My hat,
With pride.

I wear it on the farm,
I wear it in town,
I wear it because it feels good.

I don't need to be in the yards,
I don't need to be 'working',
I don't need an excuse to throw it on.

This hat is a daily reminder that I belong to something,
A community.
It's a little piece of rural life I treasure.

Some might say it's just a hat,
But it's my hat.
And even though I wear so many,
This particular one has been an anchor of sorts.

For when I've doubted my place here,
When I've questioned my contribution,
When I've wondered how on earth a former city girl like me
could survive, let alone thrive in this world . . .

This hat is always here.
I throw it on, and I feel safe.

It reminds me that I am the glue,
For my role as mother, wife and business partner
keeps the wheels turning.

This hat reminds me that rural life is home,

And I belong.

# Acknowledgements

A huge thank you to Karen, Julie McDonald, Darrylin, Pat, Danyelle, Catriona, Julie Mayne, Keelen, Sabrina, Raine, Grace, Fleur, Lyn and Diana. It has been an absolute privilege to get to know you on a deeper level and share your stories in this way.

To the Motherland community, the hundreds if not thousands of rural mums I have connected with over the past three years. Thank you for being the driving force behind this special project.

To my amazing publisher Annette Barlow who emailed me unexpectedly one day and asked me if I wanted to write this book. I'm so glad I didn't delete your email thinking it was a scam and too good to be true. I never imagined I could do this, so thank you for being my cheerleader.

To my darling husband Sam, my best friend, my teammate, my soul mate, thank you for loving me unconditionally. Our story is my favourite one of all. Thank you for supporting me with this project in every way possible so I could get to the finish line.

Finally, to our two beautiful children, Elliot and Evie: while you are still too young to read this, one day I know you will. And when that day comes, it's highly likely I'll sob rather dramatically as I explain that the two of you are the reason Motherland exists at all. Because of you, I have found so much passion and purpose while leaning into the trials and triumphs of the hardest yet most beautiful role I'll ever have . . . being your mum.

# If you'd like to know more

### Grace Brennan

Founder, Buy From The Bush

Buy From The Bush is a marketplace for Australian bush business. Think of it as your gateway to rural and regional Australia. They bring together the butchers, the bakers and the candlestick makers (of which there may not be thaaaat many) in small rural communities across Australia. They make it easy for small businesses to sell their products and for consumers to shop with purpose.

**https://www.buyfromthebush.com.au/**

### Diana Butler

CEO, Care for Africa

Care for Africa operates in rural communities in Tarime, Tanzania. Care for Africa works in five key areas: water, health, education, empowerment of women and girls, and social enterprise. At the core of the organisation's operations is an emphasis on capacity building to assist communities in breaking their cycle of poverty.

**https://careforafrica.org.au/**

### Sabrina Davis

Founder, Humans of Kangaroo Island

Since starting the project in August 2020, hundreds of stories of islanders have been told to reconnect, uplift and inspire the Kangaroo Island community and those around us. Through raw and authentic storytelling, the project managed to raise over $81,000 for the island community to recover from devastating fires and through a pandemic.

**https://humansofkangarooisland.com/**

### Danyelle Haigh

Director, Murranji Water Drilling

Murranji Water Drilling is a family owned and operated team, fully licensed, insured and experienced drillers in the construction, mining and water services with a combined experience of over 30 years.

**http://www.murranjiwaterdrilling.com.au/**

### Lyn Kelson

Founder, B 4 Motherhood

Lyn has had a career in health care over the last 35 years, as a nurse and midwife. Her goal is to equip women to have a beautiful birth on their own terms. Through bespoke education, advocacy and capacity building, Lyn's programs empower women to navigate birth systems to achieve the birth they dream of.

**https://b4motherhood.com/**

### Fleur McDonald

Author

Australia's leading rural literature author, Fleur's books become bestsellers almost as quickly as they hit the shelves. Her story lines are drawn from inspiration from having lived and worked for much of her life on farms. Loving the rural lifestyle, Fleur now owns 4050 hectares across rural Western Australia.

**https://www.fleurmcdonald.com/**

### Julie McDonald

CFO, MDH Pty Ltd.

MDH Pty Ltd is one of Australia's largest beef cattle operations, unique in the fact that the company is both family owned and operated. The McDonald family represents seven generations of beef producers and 190 years of experience in Australian agriculture.

**https://www.mdh.net.au**

### Stephanie Trethewey

Founder and CEO, Motherland

Motherland is a not-for-profit organisation and a charity that advocates for the emotional wellbeing of rural mothers. Motherland's mission is to combat the crippling isolation many rural mums face by connecting them to a supportive online community, producing a raw and relatable podcast, and offering an online mother's group program that every rural mum can access, regardless of her location.

**www.motherlandaustralia.com.au**